Betting, Booze, and Brothels

Vice, Corruption, and Justice in Jefferson County, Texas, from Spindletop to the 1960s

THE DIXIE HOTEL

THE LAW

THE TEXAS CLUB

s.telage

vice probe

"The Law West of the Neches"

Wanda A. Landrey
Laura C. O'Toole

EAKIN PRESS   Austin, Texas

*This book is dedicated to our loved ones,
whose patience, inspiration and support
over many years helped to make this book possible.*

*Floyd Landrey, Brian O Toole,
and Judy and Wayne Cerniglia*

FIRST EDITION
Copyright © 2006
By Wanda A. Landry and Laura C. O'Toole
Published in the United States of America
By Eakin Press
A Division of Sunbelt Media, Inc.
P.O. Drawer 90159 ☏ Austin, Texas 78709-0159
email: sales@eakinpress.com
☐ website: www.eakinpress.com ☐
ALL RIGHTS RESERVED.
 2   3   4   5   6   7   8   9
ISBN 978-1-57168-917-7
ISBN 1-57168-917-6
Library of Congress Control Number 2006934763

Table of Contents

Part I: The State Takes Action

Part II: Hot Times in the Old Towns

Part III: Concerned Citizens Speak Out

Part IV: The Public Hearings

Part V: The Cleanup Process

Part VI: Turning Over the Courthouse Keys

Part VII: "Doing What Comes Naturally"

Chapter 20

Part VIII: Bringing Closure

Chapter 21

Foreword

The Beaumont City Minutes for 1898 contain a petition from a group of Beaumont men who called for removal of the "houses of ill repute" along Forsythe Street, where women and children frequently shopped. The petition requested that "If [the houses] must exist in our beloved city, please force them to occupy some retired corner."

From the town's earliest years, this is the way vice was regarded in Beaumont—threatening elements might be sent to "some retired corner" in order to protect the innocent, but there was no need to eliminate them. By the turn of the twentieth century, Beaumont had acquired a reputation as a rough place, and amid the muddy, oil-soaked chaos of Spindletop, this ambivalent mindset became a self-fulfilling prophecy. For many decades, vice—gambling, prostitution, clubs that sold liquor to minors, officials who looked the other way or took money to keep quiet—simmered with growing intensity just below the surface of life in Jefferson County; then, in late 1960, it began to boil over.

From a modern perspective, the whole time seems a figment of someone's guilty nightmare. Even we Beaumonters who were there often shake our heads in disbelief as we remember the events of late 1960 and early 1961, when the Texas House of Representatives General Investigating Committee, locally known as the "James Commission," arrived in Beaumont. The Commission lost no time in beginning the "Vice Probes," as we named them, stripping away the multilayered façade of corruption, deception, and collusion from law enforcement in Jefferson County to reveal the vice beneath. We sometimes ask ourselves whether it all actually happened.

But it did happen, and the James Commission revealed another dimension—a parallel, shadow world as real as the public one, a world where brothels were an open secret to any Friday night carload of giggling high school girls driving by to spot familiar cars, and where book was made in high school cafeterias.

The James Commission's hearings were televised before an understandably enormous local audience, and for a time, mercifully brief, Jefferson County became international news. Upright, law-abiding pillars of the community rose up in righteous indignation, claiming ignorance of the entire gambling, prostitution, and illegal alcohol scene. Still, a cut-and-dried judgment was difficult to render. Even though the Vice Probes officially launched a battle between those operating within the law and those operating outside it, it could not legitimately be called a fight between good and evil; reality smudged black and white into endless shades of gray. In the final analysis, the struggle was simply a monumental growing pain, a rite of passage, a part of Jefferson County's maturation process, with many difficult lessons learned along the way.

The story of any given place is not always a pretty one; still, for the sake of history, it must be told. This singular chapter, with its trauma, high drama, low comedy, and moral lesson, has been waiting its turn for over forty years. Now, thankfully, Beaumonters Wanda Landrey and Laura O'Toole have done it. They have brought their particular skills to bear, Landrey's in historical writing and research, O'Toole's in scholarly research and legal acumen, to recreate that world of sunshine and shadow, our world as it was in 1960s Jefferson County.

Their narrative is unflinching yet affectionate. They unfold the whole story without agenda, one layer at a time, capturing not only the community's anger, frustration, and sense of betrayal at the James Commission's revelations and the subsequent chain of events, but also the inevitable episodes of comic relief. The authors respect those who were there, many of them at the dead center of the whirlwind. Fortunately, through painstaking research and countless interviews, they were able to record many memories of the various principals, according them the courtesy of speaking for themselves. And they bring to life a cast of compelling characters, among them Tom James, the fresh-faced, energetic young crusader; Charley Meyer, the powerful, gentlemanly sheriff; Ramie Griffin, the genial, party-loving district attorney; the dueling judges, Harold Clayton and Owen Lord; and Rita Ainsworth, the proprietress of the posh Crockett Street Dixie Hotel, the proverbial madam with a heart of gold who sponsored a Little League team and decorated the Dixie with poinsettias at Christmas. Public-spirited and charity-minded, "Miss Rita" looked like a society matron and became a trusted confidante of many prominent Beaumont men. For good or ill, she stands as a significant figure in Beaumont's history.

However they are regarded, the old days are gone now—but in no way forgotten. Many older Beaumonters still recall fascinating details of the Vice Probes. Even in their new life as the Crockett Street Entertainment Complex, the building façades in the 200 block of Crockett Street, the old epicenter of Beaumont's vice, evoke memories of those times, especially the Dixie Dance Hall— the old hotel's new incarnation.

And was it only coincidence that the only major storm in Beaumont's recorded history to strike the town dead-center was named—drum roll, please—"Hurricane Rita?"

—ELLEN WALKER RIENSTRA and
JUDITH WALKER LINSLEY

Acknowledgments

The authors with much appreciation and gratitude recognize the many individuals who so generously offered their assistance in helping to make this book possible. Although the manuscript is the product of the authors' joint efforts, the research was conducted at two different periods of time; therefore, they believe it appropriate to offer separate acknowledgments.

For those who assisted Wanda Landrey, she first would like to express her gratitude to the Honorable Tom James, whom she interviewed in 1996. As a young representative in the Texas House of Representatives in the early 1960s, James led the Jefferson County vice investigation and public hearings. His intriguing story of the events which transpired during his tenure prompted Landrey immediately to interview others who were involved in this fascinating era of history. To all the many people she interviewed, she offers her heartfelt thanks. As news of her interviewing project spread, she began to receive calls and letters from many others who offered their assistance. David Holstead sent her a list of interested candidates, many of whom he had already contacted. His uncle, former Jefferson County District Clerk Cecil Holstead, Tyrrell Historical Library Archivist Penny Clark, Bill Quick, Frank Messina, Roxie and Oliver Lawson, Lamar University Professor Thomas Brown, Jo Ann Stiles, John Stevens, Julia Lester, Vernon Hardcastle, and Carole Clarke also were helpful in arranging interviews. Her husband, Floyd Landrey, was of great assistance in advising her on legal matters. As time went on, interest in the authors' project was generated by related articles appearing in *The Beaumont Enterprise*, *The Beaumont Journal*, *The Examiner*, and *Triangle: The Magazine for Southeast Texas*. Former District Clerk Johnny Appleman and his staff were most helpful in making copies of a multitude of court records, and James Dishman, whose father, George Dishman, served as the first president of the United Citizens for Law Enforcement, donated his father's vast collection of documents to the project. The numerous photos loaned by Bruce Hamilton and multitude of newspaper articles shared by former state representative Lloyd Martin, who served on the General Investigating Committee of the House of Representatives, were also of much value. Archivist Clark assisted throughout the research by calling attention to related scrapbooks and numerous photographs at the Tyrrell Historical Library. Former 58th Court District Judge James Mehaffy, Judge James Farris, and Gil Rector offered valuable suggestions after reading the first draft of the manuscript; Margaret Parker always was on hand to assist with her editorial skills, as was Edna Hansford, who transcribed volumes from Landrey's recorded interviews. Last, but certainly not least, were the suggestions of Dorothy Callaway, which added creativity throughout the manuscript.

In the summer of 1987, Laura O'Toole was a senior at the University of Texas searching for a topic for her Plan II honors thesis. One evening her family was sitting around the dinner table in Beaumont and her dad suggested she do some research on the James Commission to see if that would be a good thesis topic. Although she had never heard of the "James Commission," she started looking into it and couldn't believe that after over twenty-five years no major work had been written about the incredible period in Jefferson County's history. In fact, besides newspaper archives, the only resource she found was an old scrapbook of clippings stored on a shelf at the First Methodist Church in Beaumont.

For bringing the story to life for her, and helping her graduate with honors, she gratefully acknowledges her parents, Judy and Wayne Cerniglia, and friends, Conley Todd, Mike Frank, and Donna and Paul Prince. The memories they shared of this colorful time were an inspiration and their endless patience in reading over and helping to edit the manuscript were invaluable. Their brainstorming sessions put her on the trail of many others who graciously opened their doors and took the time to tell their stories: Will Wilson, Sr., former attorney general of Texas; the Honorable Tom James for his gripping recount of the investigation and hearings that came to be known as the "James Commission;" W. T.

Wood, former assistant district attorney of Jefferson County; R. E. "Dick" Culbertson, former sheriff of Jefferson County who succeeded Charley Meyer; Mr. James Barry, son of "Huck" Barry, founding member of the United Citizens for Law Enforcement; District Judges James Mehaffy and James Farris; David Witts, former general counsel to the House of Representatives; James Vollers and Carl Kohler for insights into the grand jury process and hearings, and Jerry Conn for sharing the memories of an intrepid journalism intern at the *Beaumont Enterprise*. She is also profoundly grateful to Dr. J. M. Quinn, her supervising professor at the University of Texas, for his patient guidance and support, and the many archivists who assisted her at the Barker Texas History Center, the Tyrrell Historical Library, and the First United Methodist Church in Beaumont.

Nearly fifteen years later, she met Wanda Landrey who invited her to collaborate, and to combine their efforts into one book. She feels deeply grateful for the opportunity to have worked with Wanda. She would also like to thank Ellen Rienstra and Judy Linsley for introducing her to Wanda and for their constant support and encouragement over the years.

The authors are indebted to numerous other individuals who offered encouragement and assistance. It was indeed the combined efforts of many that resulted in the documentation of one of the most interesting eras of Jefferson County.

WANDA A. LANDREY
LAURA C. O'TOOLE

Preface

A Myth, Some Facts, and a Few Memories

The ancients tell us, and it may be true, that prostitution is the world's oldest profession. In the chronicles of time no one thought to record when it began or where it started or the names of the first practitioners. It just is. It is there, here, everywhere.

The ancients also created myths that teach us about human behavior, stories that portray the foibles and frailties of mankind, especially those related to man's longing for or his perceived need of the proverbial fruit. In long ago ages, the elders in primitive tribes used such myths to explain why Man, by his particular behavior, created so many problems for the villagers.

The myth begins with Woman, who awakened one morning with a headache and didn't feel like sponsoring her usual give-away-program. Feeling rejected and frustrated, Man sought solace and ventured into a nearby forest to meditate.

Eventually, Man became hungry, and seeing grapes hanging from a vine, he broke the vine and began to eat. Holding the grapes, he walked deeper into the forest and there he spotted Fair Maiden bathing in a brook. Desirous once again, he approached. Fair Maiden turned and, being hungry, smiled and looked longingly at his grapes . . . as Man looked longingly at Fair Maiden. Man offered to share his grapes; Fair Maiden offered to share her services . . . and the sharing began.

Soon Woman appeared and, seeing the sight before her, called Tribal Chief. He came and took Man and Fair Maiden away. Before long, Tribal Chief became hungry. So Man and Fair Maiden offered him grapes and they were set free.

As time marched on, Man and Fair Maiden exchanged money instead of grapes; Woman sometimes awakened with a headache. Man surreptitiously continued to look for the services of Fair Maiden. Fair Maiden started a business called a brothel. Tribal Chief remained in his hut as long as the money came forth. Such became the law in villages throughout the land.

Finally, many natives in the villages became disgusted after witnessing what they considered the debauching behavior of some of their fellow tribesmen. Pow-wows were held; battles were waged; new tribal chiefs were elected; the debauchees were expelled into the forest, and the moral climate within the villages improved . . . or so it appeared.

While the preceding exposé is only a fantasy, it foreshadows the story of one of the most colorful times, perhaps, in the annals of Jefferson County in southeast Texas. Man and Woman, as well as Fair Maiden and Tribal Chief, act in a symbolic manner as counterparts to the players and events in a real drama that unfolded in Jefferson County in the winter of 1960–1961.

In this era, vice activities flourished under the noses of many of the top local law enforcement officers, with their tacit approval. A swashbuckling young state legislator led state officials to conduct an intensive investigation into the rampant vice and the alleged governmental corruption that supported it. He tangled with a flamboyant sheriff and locked horns with some of the area's most powerful leaders. At a time when such things were virtually unheard of, he and his committee played it out on live television. The local governments of Jefferson County were quickly turned inside out, but it would take a persistent citizenry months of legal warfare involving a multitude of indictments, the creation of a hotly contested second district court grand jury, and debates all the way up to the Texas Supreme Court, before law and order were finally restored.

The players in this drama were real people with real names. Among the principal players one might find elected officials, concerned citizens, church leaders, businessmen, union workers, and, yes, prostitutes and gamblers. The principals played out the drama in the theater of the Jefferson County courtrooms against a backdrop of brothels, gambling halls, open-bar saloons, and private clubs where stakes were high and liquor flowed freely.

In researching the history of this fascinating era, one learns that the climate of 1960 differed little from that which had existed in Jefferson County as far back as the Spindletop boom days of early 1900. Further, it differed little from many of the other populated areas throughout Texas and the United States, for many of them also were inundated with vice and corruption by the 1920s and '30s that continued through mid-century. Just as a movement to reform the demoralizing conditions was taking place in the county in the late 1950s and early '60s, so were similar movements in existence throughout the nation.[1]

By the end of World War II, professional organized gambling and prostitution in Texas had reached an all-time high, having expanded steadily from World War I through the Depression years of the 1930s. Throughout Texas there were in excess of 75 professional dice and roulette houses, many that operated openly in luxuriously furnished quarters. Also in operation were more than 140 permanently established houses of prostitution, over 500 "bookie joints," and hundreds of agents of the numbers racket who made their living exploiting low-income groups.[2]

An increasing number of concerned citizens did voice their complaints to local and state law enforcing agencies, and the great network of professional vice operations started to crumble because of crackdowns throughout the state in such cities as Dallas, Fort Worth, and Amarillo, and the storming of Galveston in June 1957. There, state police officers blanketed the town from the plush Balinese Room to the bawdy houses on Post Office Street to the West Broadway bingo parlors.[3]

Unlike in Galveston, which shut down its vice activities, Jefferson County liquor law violations, gambling, and prostitution continued to thrive for three more years. Most citizens felt helpless to alter the situation and opted to ignore it altogether. Those who were concerned reasoned that the red-light districts in Beaumont and Port Arthur, the major cities in the county, were mainly concentrated in specific downtown areas, and the proprietors of the gambling establishments made some effort to conceal their activities. The two cities were seaport towns, and didn't the brothels, gambling clubs, and bars provide the seaman on liberty pass with the forms of recreation he sought?

The illegal operators welcomed the attitude of indifference from citizens, for it increased their profit from vice operations even though it hindered the growth of the legal economy. Many problems influenced the local economy; the city of Beaumont, alone, was $1,125,833 in the red. Other problems existed, such as high taxes, inadequate drainage and sanitary sewer systems, inconvenience and inefficiency at rail crossings, and above all, the local political situation, which greatly discouraged the expansion of industry in the community.[4]

One may at least wonder, where was the Church, whose members remained silent for so long? After all, Jefferson County was in the Southern Bible Belt with many of its citizens sitting in their pews every Sunday morning. Were some Sunday worshipers the same revelers who kicked up their heels on Saturday night? Research shows that, for many, this was true. What about the professed devout, especially ministers who failed to unite and speak out from behind their pulpits against the local vice conditions? Did they fear their words of condemnation would offend certain parishioners enough to take their membership and, therefore, their contributions elsewhere? Apparently, not even a bolt from heaven would have jolted them into action.

In the fall of 1960 the 57th Texas House of Representatives General Investigating Committee began an intensive investigation of the alleged vice and corruption activities in Jefferson County that included clandestine raids of several gambling establishments on December 3, followed by legislative committee executive hearings. During the hearings, the committee found a segment of the local community ready to cooperate. Many citizens had read articles in 1955 written by a reporter for the *Beaumont Journal* wherein he gave accounts of seeing crowds of people placing bets in gambling houses and seeing teenagers guzzling whiskey and stopping off at area brothels.[5]

The legislative committee also found organizers of the Jefferson County Grand Jury Association most cooperative. In 1955 they had founded the association after becoming alarmed over the strict control of the grand jury by the judge, the district attorney, and the sheriff.[6] Three members of the 1960 July term grand jury had taken the crusade one step farther. They initiated a plan through which they would not only work with high officials but also inform citizens of the deplorable scenes one member had witnessed when he visited various vice establishments.[7] This intense investigation led legislative committee members to decide to hold public hearings in January 1961. Only then did the committee lay out on the table details of the vice scenario and corruption in the local governments of the county, and the cleanup process began.

As I am a regional writer and historian who delights in collecting stories from people with interesting experiences, I have long been intrigued with the early vice era and its ramifications in Jefferson County. I renewed my interest when I became involved in an oral history project of Texas lawyers and I interviewed the Honorable Tom James of the Fifth District Court of Appeals in 1996. He presented such a fascinating overview of the various events that transpired during his tenure as vice chairman of the Texas House of Representatives General Investigating Committee that I decided immediately to pursue the stories of other individuals involved.

I began a search of documents that had recorded information of the historic events of 1960–61 by researching print media published at the time in local and state newspapers and magazines, chapters in books of regional interest, and court documents. The investigating committee had written a most informative report of the investigation and hearings, and I found it to be a valuable resource. I looked for and failed to find documentation of information from many of the people directly involved in the historic events, information that they, only, could tell in their own words. I concluded that those who still were around and would talk needed to have their stories recorded for posterity, even if it meant loosening the latch on Pandora's Box.

At the time I did not realize that so many people did, indeed, want to talk. From interviews with them I gleaned information that I could find from no other source. I discovered that the happenings of the time were so dramatic, so revealing, and the players so unusual and interesting that I would spend years collecting their stories and conducting other research needed to present a viable account of this important phase of Jefferson County.

In addition to persons that I interviewed, I, too, played a small part in the vice activities that led up to the investigation and hearings. As a young girl and teenager who grew up in Beaumont during the 1940s and '50s, I didn't seem to be influenced in either a positive or negative way by the red-light district and gambling halls in my town, along with the many slot machines found in almost every grocery store, restaurant, and gas station along the nearby Bolivar Peninsula. In fact, one of my fondest memories as a child was going with my family each summer for a week's vacation at the Bolivar beach. Although we spent our days playing in sand and water, we looked forward to the nightly rituals of gathering with friends at Wendy's, one of the popular hangouts. Once there, my father would pull up a chair before one of the slot machines that lined one wall so I could stand and reach the handle. He gave my sister and me a roll of nickels before he joined other adults in fellowship. We stood for at least an hour, hoping to hit the jackpot. Although I never remember my machine paying off more than an occasional two or three nickels, it was wonderful entertainment—and the perfect babysitter for our parents. We had no thoughts about engaging in an illegal activity. It was what we did when we went to the beach, but we were in church with our family on the following Sunday just the same.

When I became older and bolder, the night life on Crockett Street, which was the center of the "district" in Beaumont, became very intriguing to my friends and me. In fact, one foggy night when we were in high school, we decided to drive down just to see the action. When we entered the area, we immediately were amazed at how dark and sinister the street looked, giving us each a feeling of foreboding. We saw only a few dim lights burning that we surmised marked the much-talked about brothels in the red-light district. We gazed through the gloomy atmosphere that surrounded us only to realize the place was teeming with mysterious-looking silhouettes ambling slowly along the sidewalks. As the driver of our car slowed, we lowered the windows, and soon we heard random laughter along with an occasional jeer and catcall. In our adventure we had hoped to detect at least one or two male voices from our school so that we might spread the news to our fellow classmates, but we were disappointed not to recognize any familiar voices. We looked more intently, but before even one distinguishable figure came into focus, the car sputtered, jumped, and stopped! Frantically, our driver tried repeatedly to start the car, while we all sat with hearts pounding, right in the middle of the night, right in the middle of the road, right in the middle of the red-light district!

We could not leave the car to seek help, for one of us might be recognized, a nice girl on a "see and tell" snooping expedition. Fortunately some guys from another school, noticing damsels in distress, offered assistance. We laughed at the attention we received as one "knight in shining armor" jumped into the car, quickly started the engine, and graciously stepped back out. In a show of appreciation, we waved and blew kisses to the guys before speeding away to the safer side of the tracks.

Just as my one-time ride down Crockett Street didn't influence me to become a "hooker," neither did my mistake of entering the Liberal Club on Orleans Street one Saturday afternoon to make a telephone call cause me to take up gambling. In my mind I still can see several elderly men at tables playing dominos while others played pool, all engulfed in a cloud of blue smoke. Someone had stuffed what appeared to be pornographic literature into an old magazine rack, which hung on a wall under a chalkboard, scribbled with numbers, apparently the score from some baseball game. Since it certainly didn't look like the ideal place to spend a leisurely Saturday afternoon, much less make even one phone call, I quickly stumbled out the door, coughing all the way.

In all my naivete, even as I grew older, I simply thought that commercialized prostitution and gambling, which seemed to be common in most of the larger Texas towns, were necessary evils, not vices that violated the laws of Texas. Our police officers and county officials, I assumed, would never condone activities that were illegal. Our popular sheriff, a true straight shooter, reigned supreme over the local political arena. He stood ready to help his constituents anytime, anywhere. He also was popular with law officers over the state and served as president of the Texas Sheriff's Association. Of course, sometimes he did go overboard a bit when he loaned the college fraternity brothers at Lamar State College of Technology X-rated movies for their smokers. In high school, my civics class teacher presented the duties and responsibilities of elected officials, and I assumed that once they gave an oath to uphold the law, they did just that.

Although I played only a minor role in the drama that eventually became the historic investigation, the people I interviewed held major roles and commanded star attention. I have included many of their stories, for they add authenticity and color to the drama.

As I plodded along the research trail, I eventually heard that Laura Cerniglia O'Toole, an attorney in Austin and native of Beaumont, had written an honors thesis entitled *Purging a Corrupt Government: The Clean-up of Jefferson County* when she was a student at the University of Texas. Her thesis focused on the investigation and hearing, and she hoped to expand it one day into a book. I contacted her, and, to make a long story short, we met and decided to combine our research materials and to collaborate on writing this book.

Throughout the book we have included many personal accounts from individuals that contain explicit language. Our intention is neither to shock nor offend, but rather to present the memories of individuals in their own language as recorded during interviews with them. Their words help to portray the spirit and flavor of the times. Neither is it our purpose to present an interpretive history to change the way people view the varied institutions of vice. It is our desire, however, to add to our readers' canon of knowledge by showing how vice and corruption developed in Jefferson County in the early years of the twentieth century. And, more importantly, we hope to show how the citizens of the early 1960s attempted to use political justice to bring corruption and vice to an end.

So, now, with material derived from the Texas House of Representatives General Investigating Committee Report, Jefferson County court records, numerous newspaper and magazine articles, and the colorful accounts of more than 70 players in this most eventful field of local history, we offer this story.

—WANDA A. LANDREY

PART I

The State Takes Action

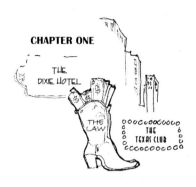

CHAPTER ONE

The Politics of Vice

Brothels! Bordellos! Red-light districts! From the beginning of time to the present, the public has acknowledged that these places exist and, subsequently, has accepted social behaviors by individuals within the confines of these locales. From the dens of inequity in old Babylon to the salons operated by sophisticated courtesans in nineteenth century France, and on to the tea houses of Japan where geisha hosted men in their "Floating World," diverse public officials have condoned, and even designated, specific places for the practice of the world's oldest profession.

By the beginning of the twentieth century, most of the larger cities in Texas, at one time or another, had a vice district encompassing several city blocks. Because such "districts" could keep the nuisance contained, most local governments and business leaders condoned prostitution in certain conditions, and efforts to mount reform movements were largely unsuccessful.

As the first World War wound down, and women's church groups and temperance leagues gained more of a voice, crusades to eliminate prostitution and illegal gambling gained steam. Anti-prostitution groups waged a sustained and successful campaign resulting in the shut-down of vice operations in Dallas, Austin, and Amarillo.[1]

During the Depression years of the 1930s, the prostitution

3

trade picked up again as crusades gave way to hunger. Once more, tolerance by law enforcement officers was the only practical response to the persistent industries of vice. Sheriff's deputies and police blinked, or perhaps winked, and looked the other way. Yet the rise of venereal disease in the booming post-World War II years spurred cities to again attempt a crackdown. Although Dallas officials tolerated prostitution at a moderate level, Houston authorities successfully instituted a policy of repression during the 1950s and officials in Corpus Christi, Harlingen, Amarillo, and Lubbock followed suit.[2]

Vice zones in other cities survived the assault, however, as entrenched political groups, some policemen, many businessmen, and liquor and vice interests staunchly backed the districts. Periodic efforts to crack down on prostitution in Beaumont and Port Arthur were short-lived and often only for show. Local supporters contended that eliminating vice districts would only disperse prostitutes into other parts of town beyond the control of police.[3]

The situation was particularly entrenched in Galveston. "If God couldn't stop prostitution, why should I?" asked the mayor of Galveston. By mid-century, leaders in Galveston's vice industry had convinced the mayor, the police department and most of the citizenry that the city's economy depended on maintaining a reputation for unimpeded gambling, drinking, and prostitution. Despite being in the "Bible Belt," many thought gambling would one day be legalized in Texas, and that Galveston could become the Las Vegas of the south. In 1955, a leading anti-prostitution organization branded Galveston the "worst spot in the nation as far as prostitution is concerned."[4]

By the late fifties, halting such political corruption and organized crime was all the rage and had become a springboard to political significance. Robert Kennedy had gained tremendous nationwide stature as chief counsel for the Senate Rackets Committee investigating corruption. As United States Attorney General, he mounted a fierce campaign to fight organized crime resulting in an 800 percent increase in convictions against organized crime figures.[5]

In Texas, a former Dallas County district attorney named Will Wilson resigned from the Supreme Court of Texas to run for Texas Attorney General. He pledged that if elected he would make every effort to stamp out vice in Galveston as well as every other county in Texas.[6] Wilson ran a successful campaign, and he began to work immediately after he took the oath of office. He brought in the famous Texas Rangers to work undercover in conjunction with his office. Together they organized raids on popular Galveston gambling establishments. These resulted in injunctions to close 47 clubs, bingo halls and brothels for "openly and flagrantly violating the laws of Texas." The Rangers smashed slot machines with ten-pound sledge hammers, burned them and dumped them into Galveston Bay.[7] Historic gambling establishments located along the beach felt the waves hit the shore.

With pressure from Wilson, the Galveston County district attorney pressed countless felony charges, and the Rangers continued their relentless assault to rid the county of any shred of gambling paraphernalia. In the aftermath, Will Wilson rode his reputation as a crime fighter to political "super-stardom" in Texas. Even a notice posted on the padlocked door of a club on 24th Street made clear who was taking credit for this war. It read, "Closed. Will Wilson's boys was here."[8]

Tom James, a handsome, ambitious, and charismatic 30-year-old lawyer from Dallas looked on with interest. He campaigned for state representative, and voters elected him to the Texas Legislature in 1958. He fully supported Wilson's "vice cleanup" project in Galveston and hoped to expand his campaign across the state. The legislature designated James as vice chairman of the 57th Texas House of Representatives General Investigating Committee charged with investigating vice conditions in Jefferson County. James jumped at the opportunity to make the cleanup of Jefferson County his claim to fame and the foundation for what he hoped to be a great political career in Texas. He soon would discover, however, that his path would not be as smooth as the road Wilson had followed.

The politically savvy Wilson, whose efforts in Galveston were met with wide praise, seemed to know just how far to push the envelope of legal reform without ruffling the wrong feathers. Wilson's political operatives, feeling the waters in Jefferson County in anticipation of a possible run at the governor's mansion, reported to the attorney general that local law enforcement officials in Beaumont were well aware of the presence of vice in their community.

However, local officials told Wilson's operatives that vice conditions in Beaumont, unlike Galveston, were "the quietest in history, small local operations of no consequence." They described Beaumont's gambling scene as "clean, honest, innocent, small stuff." Based on these reports and cognizant of the community's great affection for its powerful sheriff, Charley Meyer, Wilson kept his distance from Jefferson County.[9]

Other state politicians understood the potential Pandora's Box looming in Jefferson County and the possible ramifications from exposing its long entrenched vice "containment strategy." Many local political and business leaders undoubtably feared having their names connected to others whose activities may have been viewed with less tolerance in this new era of criminal reform. They strongly discouraged James from pursuing his mission with such fervor. Indicating that conditions in Jefferson County were much too entrenched to be changed, House Speaker Waggoner Carr told James, "You're hurting me, and you're hurting yourself." Likewise, local State Senator Jep Fuller warned the young representative, "You're not going to change any of this."[10]

Undaunted by such warnings, James was apparently willing to risk his political life. He threw himself into ferreting out illicit gambling and prostitution in Jefferson County with the zeal of a Roman gladiator. So great was his mission that locals began to refer to the investigation as the "James Commission." During the two months that followed, James and his fellow legislative committee members, Chairman Menton Murray of Harlingen, Lloyd G. Martin of Normangee, Charles Ballman of Borger, John Allen of Longview, and House General Counsel David Witts of Dallas came to realize just how complicated and explosive the situation had become.[11]

Former representative Tom James as he appeared in December 1960. James served as vice chairman of the Texas House of Representatives General Investigating Committee, which conducted the investigation of vice activities in Jefferson County in 1960-61.

—Courtesy the Austin History Center, Austin Public Library, AS 61-30262 1.

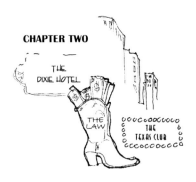

CHAPTER TWO

December 3, 1960

The Day It Rained
On the Gamblers' Parade

Three main roads connect the towns of Beaumont and Port Arthur, the two major cities of Jefferson County. Lined with industrial sites and oil refineries, none can be called scenic drives, but the unfamiliar traveler may view with interest the vast prison system that borders Highway 69 and numerous businesses along Twin City Highway. To the west of both highways is the road less traveled, known as the old Port Arthur Road. It leads past the Plum Nearly Ranch, an Arabian horse ranch owned by Jean and Gus McFaddin. Named after an employee who referred to its location as "plum nearly out of Beaumont and plum nearly to Port Arthur," long-time residents well remember that it once was the location of the Pen Yan Club, the best little casino in Jefferson County. In the 1940s and '50s, years before the McFaddins bought the property, L. L. (Jack) Thompson offered free drinks and delectable steaks to wagering patrons who checked through security. Thompson was no different from other vice operators in the county. All were under the

8

protection of the top local enforcement officials and thumbed their noses at the laws of Texas.[1]

As though this symbolic gesture was a final salute, on December 3, 1960, the Department of Public Safety officers, the Texas Rangers, and members of the 57th Texas House of Representatives General Investigating Committee targeted the Pen Yan Club and carried out the first serious vice raid ever to be conducted in Jefferson County. Their dramatic actions on that day served as a blatant announcement to all illegal practitioners that the jig was up.[2]

The investigating committee had done its homework well, and the raiding party knew what to expect. Two months earlier the committee had met in Austin to discuss the Jefferson County situation. In November 1960, after receiving a detailed report of the existing vice conditions in Jefferson County from a group of concerned citizens, the committee took the investigation into the field. Although committee members initially relied on agents from the Department of Public Safety, they insisted on going undercover themselves.[3]

Counselor David Witts recalled that he dressed like he just came off a ship. When he knocked on the door of the Pen Yan Club, a man opened the peephole and said, "Hurry up and get in; those state investigators are in town." Witts acquiesced and gave his address as being on a Mobil Oil tanker. Later he received a postcard forwarded to him from someone at Mobil signed "From all your friends at Betty's Place."[4] The committee members found flourishing in Jefferson County "the oldest, largest, and best organized vice operation in Texas,"[5] something starkly different from descriptions relayed to Will Wilson just a few years before. The officers rejoiced, for they had hit pay dirt, a second Lucas Gusher!

Witts remembered it was business as usual at the Pen Yan Club that Saturday morning, December 3, until several DPS men drifted in around 1 A.M. and casually halted a large dice game in progress. Others in the raiding party marched down the hallway toward the main room of the casino. "At the signal," Witts recalled, "I could hear Newt Humphreys announce in a loud voice, 'State Police! Everybody freeze! You're under arrest!'"[6] A bolt of lightning could not have immobilized guests in the Pen Yan Club any quicker.

After making thirty arrests, the state police called the sheriff's office for assistance to escort those arrested to the courthouse. To their surprise, Sheriff Charley Meyer responded that transportation for such a task was "unavailable." The arresting officers had no choice but to form an "honor guard" procession. They asked all those arrested to drive their own cars to the courthouse behind a lone patrol car. An officer in another patrol car brought up the rear and herded those drivers who "found it difficult not to lose their way."[7]

W. T. Wood, an assistant district attorney at the time, received a phone call about 2 A.M. from a Texas Ranger at the courthouse, who demanded that he come help with the arrests. When Wood arrived, he found the basement courthouse filled with dozens of people and countless boxes, overflowing with gambling paraphernalia and money. The raiders then asked Wood to type, one by one, complaints charging all the citizens who had participated in or simply observed activities within the club.[8] Local authorities informed state officials that facilities were unavailable to fingerprint or photograph, and a DPS photographer took "mugshots" of those arrested. All entered a plea of guilty and were released after Jack Thompson, the owner of the Pen Yan, paid their cash fines.[9]

It was not until events began to unfold later in the day that many of the top local law officials and club owners realized that their futures might be in jeopardy. DPS officers and the Texas Rangers simply looked at routine raids on clubs as common practice, all in a day's work. From time to time Port Arthur officers arrested and locked up prostitutes and madams for a few hours, primarily as a warning. Likewise they confiscated bottles of liquor from area clubs, even though they soon returned them to the clubs, unopened.

One man, who enjoyed playing dominoes in some of the Beaumont clubs during the Depression, recalled how disappointed he was when he found all the gambling operations shut down. "Don't worry about it," one of the club owners said. "We'll be open in two weeks." And sure enough, the clubs were back in business two weeks later.[10]

Raymond Lefkowitz, a freelance gambler and manager of the Balinese Club on College Street in Beaumont in 1960, was one of the first to learn of the early morning raid at the Pen Yan. He was surprised to see Tex Phillips, the security guard at the Pen Yan

Club, at the Kitten Coffee Shop so early in the morning. Phillips reported, "We got knocked off tonight." Both men had seen raids before. But this raid, they agreed, was different. By 1:30 that afternoon DPS officers, Texas Rangers, and House Committee members launched another raid on six clubs in downtown Beaumont, and Lefkowitz knew things were about to change for good.[11]

Having visited the establishments on more than one occasion, the agents and raiding officers were familiar with all the popular gambling spots. In each club, there was basically the same equipment: Daily Racing Forms, *Chicago Turf Bulletin*, scratch sheets, and odds on horse racing and sporting events throughout the country. In the corner of each gambling club was a Western Union ticker tape machine faithfully issuing its information on sporting events. A bookie stood behind a counter ready to do business in front of a large tote board on which he wrote or posted wagering information.[12]

Many of the younger members of the Beaumont Police Department were just as surprised as the gamblers to learn of the afternoon raids of the Beaumont clubs. "It was all hush-hush," said Charles Perricone, a third-year veteran. "The first I knew of it, I was sent out to check on a stolen car when I got a call on the radio, saying, 'Get back in here.' I was thinking, 'What have I done?' When I got there, off we went. Since I was working in the Identification Department, my job was to take pictures of the different gambling places."[13]

On signal, the raiders invaded the six Beaumont clubs—the Bowie Club, the Liberal Club, Rich's Club, the Commodore Club, the Texas Club, and the Yukon Club. At each club arresting officers were able to make bets necessary to complete their case prior to an arrest. One committee member found himself greeted by a zealous bookie who shoved a daily racing form into his hand and said, "What'll you have?" before the arresting officer could say, "You're under arrest!"[14]

Joe Perl, a popular and well-known Beaumont realtor, recalled the afternoon in vivid detail. He walked out of his office to Crockett Street after he heard sirens blasting. There he saw the Texas Rangers getting out of their cars. They walked into the Texas Club and found a young man standing on a ladder, which rotated all around the walls so he could post the results of horse races.

When the young man saw the first Ranger coming in, he jumped off the ladder and ran. Perl remembered he ran "faster than the horses he was marking."[15]

By about 2:30 that afternoon, the various raiding parties had confiscated a great deal of gambling paraphernalia, approximately $16,000 in cash, and literally hundreds of pounds of bookmaking and wagering equipment. As they began their trek to the courthouse, the local law enforcement agencies again offered no assistance to the state officers. Like they had after the Pen Yan raid, officers requested those arrested to form an "honor guard" and trusted the gamblers to comply.

A plain-clothes officer asked one of the club operators, who held a box filled with gambling equipment, to ride in a taxi with him. When they told the driver where to take them, the driver prophetically asked, "Are you guys taking your Christmas presents down early?"[16]

Officers found an interesting item among the paraphernalia they confiscated at the Bowie Club, a "tally book" that listed many names, one of which was "Charley Meyer." When investigators questioned the operator about the name, he stated that he didn't know who Meyer was but thought he was a bartender at the Cricket Club. Investigators then checked the Beaumont telephone directory and found only one Charles Meyer, the sheriff of Jefferson County. When officers observed another entry as "R.G.," they asked the operator if the initials could stand for Ramie Griffin, the district attorney. The operator confirmed their query and stated that on occasion "Ramie Griffin has stopped in and had a few drinks." But since he is not a member of the club, the operator added, "his drinks were free."[17]

In the 1950s, Jack Thompson operated the Pen Yan Club between Beaumont and Port Arthur on the old Port Arthur Road. Today the property is known as the Plum Nearly Ranch, owned by Jean and Gus McFaddin.

—The Wanda A. Landrey collection, Courtesy the Tyrrell Historical Library

Gambling chips and a die found by Jean McFaddin in a flower bed on the Plum Nearly Ranch.

—Courtesy Jean McFaddin

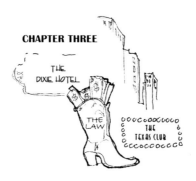

CHAPTER THREE

THE
DIXIE HOTEL

THE
LAW

THE
TEXAS CLUB

Charley Meyer and Ramie Griffin

Few characters in this tale of Jefferson County's colorful past capture the flavor of the times better than its celebrated sheriff and dashing district attorney. Exceptionally charismatic and always wearing a western hat and cowboy boots, Charley Meyer reigned over the political scene in Jefferson County with a John Wayne swagger. He exhibited the manners of a southern gentleman and the grit of a frontiersman. And for most of his 16-year tenure, the people of Jefferson County trusted him and thought he could do no wrong.

Born on February 14, 1913, in the small town of Ellinger, Texas, located halfway between LaGrange and Columbus on Highway 71, Meyer studied business administration at Texas A&M and graduated in 1934 before he embarked on a storied law enforcement career.[1] He first distinguished himself in southeast Texas as an outstanding Texas Department of Public Safety trooper when he helped Jefferson and Hardin County officers hunt down noted Texas desperado Thomas Jefferson "Red" Golemon. The outlaw hid in the East Texas Big Thicket for months before officers discovered him and ordered him to surrender. Golemon was shot and killed when he refused to surrender.[2]

In 1941 the Japanese bombed Pearl Harbor, and Meyer, like other young men, entered the U.S. Army where he gained hero

14

status as 2nd Lt. C. H. Meyer. Seeing fierce action in the jungles of New Guinea and the Philippines, Meyer spent three years overseas without leave and suffered six bouts with malaria. He accepted an honorable discharge in February 1945 after four years of service during which he readily reached the rank of lieutenant colonel and commanded a special troop battalion. The U.S. Army honored him with a Bronze Star, five battle stars, and a unit citation.[3]

Meyer was eager to get back into law enforcement upon his return from the battlefields. In 1946 he joined a slate of eight other men vying for the job of Jefferson County sheriff. He won in a runoff against Jim Stafford and took office on January 1, 1947. Meyer inherited a way of law enforcement that operated more from a common sense perspective than the strict rule of law. In his territory of Jefferson County, Meyer ruled it the way he saw fit. "It was the kind of law enforcement people had expected since Spindletop," recalled Dick Culbertson, who served as sheriff after Meyer. "When it came to crimes like murder and rape, Charley did extremely well."[4] He dealt with gambling and prostitution, on the other hand, in an entirely different fashion. Meyer, himself, explained his lack of attention to the problems of vice as "selective enforcement," and he insisted that he could better spend limited manpower on real crimes. Meyer and Jim Mulligan, the Beaumont police chief, like their predecessors, were resigned to the fact that vice would always prevail. Beaumont was, after all, a port town. They subscribed to the traditional point of view, that prostitution was a necessary evil, and they truly seemed to believe it protected the women from marauding rapists and sailors who'd been at sea too long. Rather than turn a blind eye, however, Meyer and others sought to regulate the trade, believing that controlling measures they put in place could contain the vice and manage the darker elements that came with it. "I think the houses of prostitution were for a good purpose," said Leonard Hamm, a former deputy sheriff who served under Meyer and as head of the vice department under Mulligan. "Back in those days, you didn't hear about women being pulled off the streets and being raped or all those venereal diseases that are out there now. Those sailors and guys had a place to go."[5]

Meyer exerted considerable influence over the grand juries who considered any charges brought before them by local law enforcement. During his time in office, no grand jury ever returned an indictment against a gambler or prostitute. Meyer made sure his intentions in this regard were well understood by grand jurors, who were selected repeatedly from a list he helped create. With his incredible charm, he presented each of them with a star shaped badge on which the juror's name appeared. Each badge signified that juror as an "honorary deputy sheriff." After the jurors completed their sessions of duty, assuming all went to Meyer's satisfaction, he, Criminal District Judge Owen M. Lord, or District Attorney Ramie Griffin served as host and entertained them at a party.[6]

Even after all the revelations in the public hearings about liberties taken by the sheriff with regard to vice in their city, the people of Jefferson County still adored Charley Meyer. At the conclusion of the hearings, the investigating committee published a report of their findings. The public read the report and fully understood the serious allegations against their sheriff. Months after the investigative hearings concluded, Hurricane Carla smashed into the Gulf Coast and claimed many lives. In response to Meyer's efforts, the battered public praised their heroic sheriff in numerous letters to the *Beaumont Enterprise*. "Thank you, Charley, for the many great jobs you have done . . . Good luck to our good sheriff."[7] The affable sheriff took in even Tom James, whose efforts saw the permanent end to Meyer's career in law enforcement. "He was a marvelous rogue," James said. "I never felt any ill will toward him."[8]

If Charley Meyer was the picture of a southern gentleman, District Attorney Ramie Griffin balanced the ticket with his reputation as a fun-loving party guy. Born in the East Texas sawmill town of Bessmay, Ramie inherited the dark, striking features of his father, "Black" Frank Griffin, so named because of his Native American heritage. An apothecary with no formal licensing, Frank moved the family from one small East Texas town to another buying and selling failing drugstores for profit. They finally settled in Liberty, where Frank successfully ran Griffin's Drugstore and served as mayor.

After he graduated from Liberty High School, Ramie attended the University of Texas and obtained his law degree from Baylor Law School. While at Baylor, he roomed with Abner McCall, who eventually became president of the university. Following law school, Ramie served in the Judge Advocates Corps during World War II. He then returned to the area to practice law in Liberty and

Freeport before moving to Beaumont. Here he worked as an assistant district attorney under Jefferson County District Attorney Jep Fuller. When Fuller decided to run for the Texas Senate in 1950, Ramie jumped at the chance to take his place as District Attorney. Both politicians were successful in their bids.[9]

Intelligent and extremely handsome with thick black hair and piercing blue eyes, the personable Ramie Griffin made friends easily and never met a stranger. He exhibited a personality that drew people to him, and, in return, he genuinely seemed to care about them. The dashing DA's favorite pastime when he wasn't fishing was to show off his considerable skills at gin rummy.[10]

According to his son, Ramie, Jr., Griffin entertained the idea of trying to close down gambling and prostitution that flourished when he first took office. Instead, he listened to his two brothers, a doctor and a pharmacist, who urged him to leave well enough alone. They thought the political ramifications might be too great, especially with his predecessor, Jep Fuller, climbing the political ranks in the Texas Senate.[11] Ramie Griffin reluctantly decided to comply with the system he inherited. He played a hand that ended his political career.

Charley Meyer and Ramie Griffin each found a comfortable niche within the political arena at a time when vice spun out of control. They observed the climate and found an easy way to deal with the problems they found in Jefferson County.

Like a sea change, the news generated by the raids on the Pen Yan and other clubs set in motion a series of events that influenced the futures of many elected officials and also galvanized the citizens of Jefferson County to work for changes in attitudes and social behaviors.

Charley Meyer, who served as Jefferson County's popular sheriff during the hustling and bustling days of the 1940s and '50s, was caught in the web of political reform in the early 1960s.
—*Courtesy* the Tyrrell Historical Library

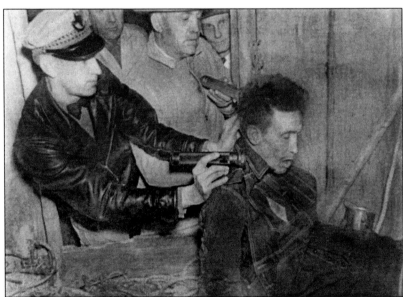

As a young Texas DPS trooper, Charley Meyer first gained recognition as a fearless officer of the law when he assisted Jefferson and Hardin County officials in apprehending and killing noted Texas outlaw Thomas Jefferson "Red" Golemon in the Big Thicket on April 11, 1940.
—Photo appeared in *Outlaws in the Big Thicket.*
Courtesy Eakin Press

*District Attorney Ramie
Griffin in the 1950s.*
—Courtesy Ramie
Griffin, Jr.

*In a skit at a Jefferson County Bar Association party in the 1950s, Attorney Al Gerson
dressed as television adventure character "Ramor of the Jungle" to lampoon District
Attorney Ramie Griffin, demonstrating his partying spirit.*
—Courtesy Judge Al Gerson

CHAPTER FOUR

THE
DIXIE HOTEL

THE
LAW

THE
TEXAS CLUB

Initial Reactions

As news of the December 3, 1960, raids spread throughout the southeast Texas community, public reaction soared, especially after the investigating committee issued the following statement:

> We are here to investigate charges largely substantiated by the raids made Saturday that vice, narcotics, gambling and liquor law violations are flourishing in this area under circumstances that indicate virtual immunity from prosecution. If your laws are inadequate, they must be strengthened. If our state agencies have failed to act, we want to know why. If local law enforcement is not functioning, we want to know what the Legislature should do to help those citizens who respect the laws and are entitled to have them enforced. From evidence obtained from the raids conducted by undercover agents working with the committee, it is apparent that vice operations here are the oldest, largest and most thoroughly organized in the state.[1]

Upon hearing the news of the raids and the House Committee statement, many members of the Beaumont Police Department were relieved that the crackdown had begun. Gene Corder, a patrol officer in 1960, said he loved every minute of the downtown raids. Having felt frustrated and helpless for years about the internal operations within the department, he had been looking for employment elsewhere and was waiting for calls from several area refineries when the raids occurred. Regarding prostitution and gambling in Beaumont, Corder indicated that he and others among the rank and file were given the following orders: "Do not go in, do not go around, do not associate, do not acknowledge." Should an officer do otherwise, he would be fired.[2]

Corder exhibited a feeling of frustration that was apparent to Officer Cecil Rush while they patrolled the downtown streets of Beaumont one evening. He recalled that two women wrecked their car and Officer Rush arrested them for failure to carry a driver's license. At the police station, Corder asked one of the women where she lived. To his dismay, she gave as her address one of the local brothels. When he asked the woman to state her occupation, she responded angrily, "I'm a housewife, dummy!" Cecil Rush turned to his partner and made a prediction. He explained that the booking officer would release them before he and his partner could get out the door. "Sure enough, that's what happened," Corder remembered. "One phone call and they were gone."[3]

Patrolman John Parsons, who shared Corder's disenchantment with the Beaumont Police Department, was in Tennessee negotiating to buy a farm when the raids came. Parsons' decision to find employment elsewhere came as the result of a humiliating incident that occurred while he was also trying to perform his duties. The incident was precipitated by what Parsons considered the deplorable behavior of one of his superior officers.

According to Parsons, it was a common occurrence for young policemen in the department to be "set up" with prostitutes by a superior, a strategy which gave police management more control. Parson's experience with the "strategy" later cost his boss his job. He was working evenings with Frank Haley, a newly promoted detective. Haley and Parsons were called by the chief of detectives to go to the Marine Hotel, a big old green building on Tevis Street in Beaumont. The men went to the appointed place and waited for the chief, thinking it was unusual for him to send them to a known brothel. When he arrived, Haley and Parsons greeted him and followed him into a little dining area. In came the madam and all the girls, Parsons recalled, about five or six in all. Once seated at the dining table, the chief began to question the girls about the "business details" of their trade. He asked them where they were from, whether they had a pimp, and how long they'd been plying their trades. Satisfied, he turned to the befuddled officers and said "Hey, Parsons, you and Haley pick you a couple of girls and go on upstairs." Parsons, red-faced, stammered, "I don't believe so, thank you." He spun around to look at Haley who was "glowing like a stop sign." Again, the superior officer ordered the two young officers to go upstairs with the understanding that the services were compliments of the house. Both men again declined and got up to leave. The chief commented as they were walking out the door, "I got a theory, Parsons. If a guy won't f___, he won't fight." At that point, Parsons had had enough. "Chief," he said, "that kind of business is not what I do. Now if you think I won't fight, you just jump whenever you feel 'froggy.'" His boss smiled coolly. "Kid," he retorted, "I was just trying to rile you up."[4]

Three of the top local law enforcement officials were not as pleased as Beaumont police officers Corder and Parsons to hear that Representative James was taking control of the vice conditions in Jefferson County. Sheriff Charley Meyer and District Attorney Ramie Griffin challenged the statements made by James as an exaggeration, especially the allegations of a flourishing narcotics traffic in the county. Garland Douglas, chief of police in Port Arthur, replied that no organized commercial gambling had existed in his city for a long time. Douglas insisted that he gave his men standing orders to break up any gambling if they found it, and that they had managed to wipe out all houses of prostitution that had operated in the past.[5]

Griffin, reacting strongly to having his turf trod upon by the upstart legislator, immediately announced that he intended to have James called before the Jefferson County grand jury for questioning on December 13. Notified of this "invitation" at his home office in Dallas on December 8, James eagerly accepted. He alleged, however, that the grand jury invitation was a "bush-league trick to sweep under the rug facts which would be made public." Since grand juries convened only in closed session, James doubted it would cooperate with the very public effort to inform the citizens about the problems of vice."[6]

Just days before his date with the grand jury, James and his committee members met in Austin. At the meeting, they agreed to pursue a full-scale investigation of alleged vice conditions in the

Beaumont area. They also decided to involve the Texas Attorney General's office by requesting an investigation into whether Western Union violated a permanent injunction prohibiting it from supplying its services for bookmaking.[7] Will Wilson found his office involved in Jefferson County's affairs after all.

Jim Mulligan, the Beaumont police chief, also reacted quickly to the news of the December 3 raids and Representative James' report. In an effort to demonstrate his police department's intentions to wipe out gambling, he stated, "The lid is on," and immediately announced that he would seek funds to establish a permanent vice squad to enforce the city's gambling and prostitution laws.[8]

As early as December 7, the *Beaumont Enterprise* noted that "the blackout of vice spots in Beaumont was described by longtime observers as the most total shutdown within memory," and that "the neon signs in front of five hotels between the Neches River and Orange Street were turned off." The newspaper further stated that "At one of the hotels a sign on the front screen door read 'On vacation.'" Police Chief Mulligan was quoted as saying, "Residents of the hotels either have found rooms elsewhere in the city or maybe they have gone to Dallas."[9]

House Committee members gathered in Beaumont several days later to prepare to meet in executive session and found that many of the illegal operators had assumed a most flippant attitude toward the officers attempting to probe vice and corruption. The committee found that the Pen Yan Club and several other establishments that allowed gambling had closed; yet they found that prostitution and liquor law violations continued, and that the men who ran the numbers racket continued to operate.[10]

On December 20, the full House committee met in Beaumont at the Ridgewood Motel in executive session. Summoned to testify privately before the committee were many of the county's top law officers, city officials and vice operators.[11]

When District Attorney Ramie Griffin was questioned by committee members about his law enforcement techniques, he stated, "I don't want to stick my neck out if people are not interested." He also approached the subject of prostitution by saying that a seaport town "needs to have prostitution to protect our wives and daughters from rape."[12]

In response to Griffin's testimony concerning the necessity for prostitution in a seaport town, James adamantly disagreed. "It doesn't protect the community from rape and assaults. It doesn't have anything to do with it. It's an atrocity against humankind to tolerate women being subjected to that." During the executive session, he mentioned being contacted by the father of a girl in one of the houses, who had hired someone to get her out and couldn't. The father indicated that many of the girls who tried to leave were "beaten to a pulp" and some were even killed.[13]

Port Arthur City Manager Charles Brazil initially refused to cooperate with the committee members when first questioned. He declined to acknowledge any violation of the law in Port Arthur and denied knowledge of any gambling places or houses of prostitution in his city. Later, however, after the session concluded, Brazil sought out members of the committee and asked if he could make a voluntary statement. He said that just before he left his home to go to Beaumont for the hearings, he had received an anonymous phone call from a man who cautioned him to be "very, very careful what he said to the committee." Brazil, who had a wife and two daughters, interpreted this call as a threat. He had an actual fear that "someone was going to throw acid in his daughter's face."[14]

"It was indeed serious times with serious people," David Witts said:

> James and I received threatening phone calls and were told things like "for $25, I could get you guys face down in a rice paddy." We had a DPS bodyguard, who slept in the room with us at all times. One time somebody opened the door and threw something in that looked like a bomb, but, fortunately, it wasn't. It was dressed up, taped and wired, and looked like one.[15]

On a lighter note, Representative Lloyd Martin recalled that one of the DPS men, who had sat in on the hearing in which Meyer was questioned in executive session, commented that he had known Charley Meyer many years and had never seen him wear anything but cowboy boots. But on the day that he was questioned, he sported a new pair of tailored shoes. "Did you notice today that Charley was wearing a new pair of shoes?" the agent asked the committee members. "I bet he bought those shoes just to come here and meet with you, because he knows y'all aren't cowboys."[16]

The committee members must have found amusing another event in which Beaumont Police Chief Jim Mulligan "took action" and launched a crusade against church bingo and American Legion raffles. Mulligan sent armed deputies out on a raid. They seized a punch board from a local fund-raiser used to raffle off a five-pound box of chocolates.[17] In a report to the *Beaumont Enterprise*, Representative James quickly addressed Mulligan's "raid" in the press, saying:

> If Chief Mulligan thinks that this is the source of crime and vice in Jefferson County, we hold little hope that effective enforcement will come under his administration.
>
> The problem that should attract his attention is not in the churches. It is the phony membership clubs, and in the bawdy houses, and in the bookie joints.[18]

Following the lead of a "whistle blower," who had previously testified about substantial pay-offs to certain area officials, James called a press conference and subpoenaed copies of most of the witnesses' income tax forms. James took a chance that the witnesses asked to appear before his committee would respect the IRS more than the state of Texas. He later explained his motives:

> It was a total bluff. If anyone had balked, I don't think we would have done the public hearings. You see, our committee would have expired when the next legislative session started in January. It would have taken too many witnesses and too much time.
>
> We knew that Charley Meyer had been convicted earlier of income tax evasion, so everyone would have been afraid not to list their [campaign] contributions. It worked! Once we had their sworn income tax returns, it only left the question of why the officials got the money and how it was given to them.[19]

At the close of the two-day session some of the committee members prepared to return to their homes. In spite of the few ominous threats that members reported, the committee received an overwhelming outpouring of encouragement from concerned citizens throughout the community.

By late December, it was quite apparent that the extent of the problem in Jefferson County went far beyond gambling, prostitution, and a little narcotics traffic. The General Legislative Investigating Committee had collected a tremendous amount of information over the last two months. Committee members took note of both the information and genuine concern expressed by many members of the community. They formulated a plan that would inform the public of the cancer that festered within. Just before New Years Day, Representative James announced that the committee would hold three days of public hearings concerning the situation, beginning on Wednesday, January 4, 1961, in the Federal Building in Beaumont. A team of officials headed by B. L. Parker, sergeant-at-arms of the House of Representatives, with assistance from the Texas Rangers and others, commenced serving more than 100 subpoenas.[20]

The first public notice was received Sunday morning, January 1, 1961. The headlines of the *Beaumont Enterprise* read in colorful scroll, "Happy New Year." Immediately under the greeting appeared the line, "Vice Hearings Open Wednesday."[21]

Representatives James and Martin, along with Counselor Witts, returned to Beaumont early to continue the probe into the effects of wide-open vice on members of the community. Martin recalled that on January 2 the manager of the Cricket Supper Club issued them membership cards. While they were watching the floor show that evening, the guests roared as the emcee announced that "under the new Texas law, we can't do some of the things we've been doing." Everyone knew the laws hadn't been changed at all. The club simply now had to stop breaking the laws.[22]

The announcement of the impending vice hearings quickly became the talk of southeast Texas. Since all but the naïve knew that gambling and prostitution had been in and around Beaumont and Port Arthur for over half a century, most residents were skeptical that anything would change at all. But their apathetic attitudes were about to be challenged.

The hearings promised to reveal a political network that encouraged vice to flourish in Jefferson County. However, three days of hearings could not possibly capture the colorful mosaic of the county's underworld. From the flamboyant madams who operated its infamous brothels to the savvy gamblers who ran wagering operations all over town, an entire culture had thrived behind closed doors since the glory days of Spindletop. Their reputations spanned the globe and their stories became the stuff of legend.

This taped and wired object, which resembled a bomb, was thrown into the room where members of the House of Representatives General Investigating Committee met in executive session at the Ridgewood Motel in December 1960.
—Courtesy David Witts

Headlines of the Sunday Enterprise on January 1, 1961, announcing the opening of the vice hearings.

Members of the Texas House of Representatives General Investigating Committee met in executive session at the Ridgewood Motel in Beaumont in December, 1960. Seated left to right: Rep. Tom James; Rep. Lloyd G. Martin; David Witts, chief counsel for the committee; and Rep. Charles Ballman.
—Microfilm photo from the Beaumont Enterprise, December 20, 1960.
Courtesy the Beaumont Public Library

PART II

Hot Times
In the Old Towns

The discovery of oil at Spindletop Hill on January 10, 1901, ushered in the age of "black gold," and the news echoed around the globe to put the towns of Beaumont and Port Arthur on the world map. But it was the boom days' mania following Spindletop that brought in the gamblers and ladies of the night to give the two places their illicit glitter.

CHAPTER FIVE

THE
DIXIE HOTEL

THE
LAW

THE
TEXAS CLUB

The Early Beaumont "District"

A newspaper article appeared on the front page of the *Beaumont Daily Journal* on June 23, 1903, and made reference to the problems the city of Beaumont had with many of the gambling houses in the downtown area. In the article, "Mayor Langham Wants Gambling Stopped," the writer described an incident in which officers arrested four blacks in gambling establishments throughout the city and then questioned them in corporate court. The first one questioned was an employee of Charles H. Ainsworth, the owner of a gambling saloon on Buford Street. Charged with sleeping in a public place, the man testified that he had gone home, only to find the door locked, and returned to the saloon, where he fell asleep. The officers believed his story, and he escaped a fine. The officers fined the other men because they "hang about these gambling houses and late in the night prowl around and steal chickens or anything else they can make away with."[1]

Officers and clients casually called the early "red-light" district in Beaumont the "Reservation," so named because it was centered primarily in the designated area bound by Crockett, Trinity, Bonham, and Jefferson streets.[2] However, judging from the "ladies" who called out from behind Dutch doors to those passing by, there was no need for a reservation. Almost any white male between the age of early puberty and senility was welcomed . . . as long as he had the money. The dwellings were non-luxurious shotgun-type houses divided into rooms called "cribs," but were comfortable enough for any patron to have his passion satisfied. A common joke often told among longtime residents was that the crude dwellings were built close to the Oil City Brass Works, a foundry located on the corner of Crockett and Park, so that the pounding at the foundry would muffle out the pounding in the district.[3]

Beaumont physician C. L. Pentecost, who worked the night shift one summer in the early 1930s as a delivery boy for a drug store, fondly recalled trying to get an "eye full" when he delivered sandwiches and cigarettes to the houses of prostitution. "I always wanted to look and see all I could see, but the madams never let me get past the front door," he said. "If my mother had known where I was going on those night deliveries, she'd have killed me. But, I usually got a two or three dollar tip, which was a lot of money in those days. It was a profitable summer."[4]

Equally as curious about the "ladies" in the "district" was Minni Palumbo Lindsey, who lived nearby over a grocery store run by her grandparents, Tony and Lilly Molly Tortorice. As a little girl of five or six in the late '30s, she often walked with her father past the porch where a friendly madam named Eldora and about 15 or 20 very young and beautiful girls sat during the day. Minni was so impressed with Eldora, who always wore gorgeous negligees and reeked of wonderful-smelling perfume, that she would often run and sit on her lap. "She was a bleached blonde, had milky white skin, big blue eyes, and wore makeup, which was unusual back then. She wasn't cheap looking, more like a Mae West," Minni recalled. "I was too young to know what was going on, but I just knew I wanted to dress like them, smell good like them, and wear makeup like them.[5]

Proponents of red-light districts, mainly those who considered prostitution a necessary evil, were quick to mention certain attributes of the long-established system in Beaumont. For example, the Beaumont Police Department kept a watchful eye over the district and issued certain requirements for all prostitutes. Each new "girl" in town was expected to report to the police station for a "mug shot." All were required to submit to a weekly health examination and carry some evidence documenting good health; and all were expected to observe early evening curfew hours. In addition, many of the "house" proprietors served as very valuable police informants because their establishments often attracted members of the criminal population.[6]

Local attorney Tanner Hunt remembers his father, who was editor of the *Beaumont Enterprise* and the *Beaumont Journal* for many years, telling him about an incident that occurred late one night in the '30s. He received a call from a reporter who advised him of a disturbance on Crockett Street that involved Toni Jo Henry, a gun moll, who had broken her boyfriend out of jail. Officers found him holed up in one of the brothels. The boyfriend was none other than Raymond Hamilton, the infamous gangster and cohort of Bonnie and Clyde. At the time, Hamilton was a much sought-after fugitive, traveling from one part of Texas and Louisiana to another. Fatty Burrell, the police officer on duty, was apparently fearless, because he went to the brothel alone to make the arrest. He found Hamilton asleep in one of the bedrooms and captured him without any assistance.[7]

Unlike with Hamilton, police officers provided greater security for Al Capone, the notorious gangster from Chicago, when he stopped for a short time in Beaumont. Federal officers were transferring him by train from Atlanta to the West Coast, and Capone had no opportunity to visit a local brothel that night. Hunt's father recalled that the officers allowed him the privilege of interviewing Capone under heavy guard. It was an experience he would never forget.[8]

The Ainsworths Meet "Miss Rita"

Charles H. Ainsworth owned much of the real estate in the early red-light district. Buster Turner, one of the first African-American policemen hired in Beaumont, recalled that Nathaniel Ainsworth, Charles' son, kept a watchful eye over all his father's holdings to make sure everyone stayed in line. "He wore cowboy boots and sat in a rocking chair," Turner said. "If a black man walked by, he knew he better look straight ahead." According to Turner, the black prostitutes mainly met men on the streets or at a club and would take them to their houses or other people's houses. Often older divorced or widowed women, who needed extra money, would convert a room in their houses for their "guests."

Working girls called these converted rooms "transit" houses, as they would use them only for a short time. The red-light district supported an abundant number of these houses even though the owners never advertised their location.[9]

As expected, most brothel owners were very discreet about their property in the red-light district. Beaumont businessman Smythe Shepherd, who lived near the Ainsworth family as a boy, recalled that "Charles Ainsworth owned a bottling company on Bonham Street and a lot of real estate back then. I was in and out of their house often, and they seemed like a very nice family."[10] It was during the late '30s that Rita Claire Gonzales, an attractive woman in her mid-thirties, emerged on the Beaumont underworld scene and into the life of Nathaniel Ainsworth. Records show that Rita, the daughter of Lorenzo Gonzales and Alicia Lupe DeMarr, was born on September 15, 1903, in San Francisco, California.[11] Today no one knows exactly how she landed in Beaumont. People tell stories about her past that are as numberless as grains of sand in an hourglass. Bruce Hamilton, former head of the Beaumont Historical Commission, said it was his understanding that Rita was a member of a vaudeville troupe that disbanded while performing in Beaumont.[12] Other undocumented accounts describe her as a showgirl in a New York City production, as the "kept" girlfriend of a member of a prominent Chicago family, and as the wife of a man named Angel Guadarama in Mexico City.[13] Judging from the many photographs of a man named Sylvester found among her collection of memorabilia, she may have married again. People who knew her well recall that she spoke fluent Spanish and in her twenties wrote a delightful play with a Mexican theme and setting.[14]

Rita liked Beaumont enough to stay and reportedly worked "on-line" in one of Charles Ainsworth's "cribs."[15] She didn't work as a "lady of the evening" long, because in 1938 she married Charles' son, Nat, who previously had been married and divorced three times and had full custody of his children, Charles and Mary Lou.[16]

Judging from the divorce petition that Olive Knippel Ainsworth, Nat's third wife, filed on September 3, 1936, Rita probably should have checked his matrimonial track record before saying "I do." The petition alleged that the marriage ceremony of Nat and Olive "never would have been possible except for the fact that prior to and at the very time of the ceremony on the 14th day of August 1936, plaintiff and defendant were both of beastly intoxication and neither in a position to realize or know what was in fact taking place." Olive further alleged that the "defendant is an habitual drunkard and remains in a state of intoxication that wholly renders him unfit to take care of a wife and incapable of treating decently and humanely much less bestowing upon her the attention and affection that a wife deserves."[17]

Soon after Rita married Nat, she joined in the family operations. The Beaumont City Directory listed her as being in the Ainsworth's soft drink business at 793 Bonham.[18] By the summer of 1943, however, it became apparent that Nat Ainsworth just couldn't get the marriage thing right with Rita, either. On August 14, 1943, Rita filed for divorce, alleging in her petition that in spite of doing everything within her power to make their home life happy and pleasant, she was subjected to "unkind, harsh, cruel and tyrannical treatment, and that he continuously drinks."[19] Rita did go back to him, not once, but five times with the intent of making their marriage work, because five amended divorce petitions followed the original petition, all filed at the Jefferson County Courthouse between January 1944 and January 1945.[20]

In spite of their tumultuous relationship, Rita experienced at least one endearing moment after she filed her second petition. Nat was in the service of Uncle Sam, traveling by train on September 7, 1944, to Spokane, Washington. On a small piece of paper, he scribbled a note to her, and on the back wrote his will, which he airmailed to her the next day. He acknowledged that "It's a hell of a looking will, but it comes from my heart." Concerned over his children's welfare and his thoughts of possibly not returning from his tour of duty, Nat stated that he was leaving Rita all his property and money because he knew she would always care for his children in the proper way. The will was signed, "I love you always, Nat A. Ainsworth."[21]

Nat did return, but judging from the three additional divorce petitions filed by Rita, which alleged his increasingly brutal behavior, there was no hope of reconciliation. The courts never granted the divorce, and on April 23, 1947, while Nat was in the Beaumont City Jail on some charge, an officer found him dead.[22] By this time Rita had converted the upstairs into what she listed in the

Beaumont City Directory as her "coin phonograph business" at 250½ Bowie. Others would refer to the business as a brothel called the Shamrock Rooms.[23] From this unhappy union came the entrepreneurial seeds of a great business venture and perhaps the most infamous bordello in the state's history.

The War Years:
Lusty Troops Come to Town

World War II was good for business in the district. In the springs and summers of 1940 and 1941, several divisions of the United States Army convened in the area between Leesville and Shreveport, Louisiana, to conduct mock war battles called the "Louisiana Maneuvers" in preparation for the possibility of war.[24] As expected, some of the soldiers managed to maneuver their way over to visit the brothels in Beaumont.

Beaumont ear, nose and throat specialist Dr. David Sockler was taking a refresher course in Chicago in 1966, and was riding in a taxi from his classes to his hotel, when he learned that his driver had been a member of one of the divisions sent to Louisiana in 1940. The driver related to Dr. Sockler that when he was traveling in a convoy to Louisiana for maneuvers and passed through Beaumont, he and his cohorts learned of the red-light district. That night their unit stopped in Orange to spend the night, so several of the soldiers pooled their resources and found a man with a big stake-sided truck to haul them back to Beaumont for a visit. "When I got with the girl," the man told Dr. Sockler, "I asked her the price, and she said it was three dollars. So I said, 'I'll tell you what. If I give you five dollars, can I do it twice?' She said, 'Yeah, if you think you're man enough . . .' So I did."[25]

After the United States entered World War II, the army base at Fort Polk and the air force base at DeRidder, Louisiana, became centers of military activity. It was then that the Beaumont red-light district doubled in size because of the large number of soldiers visiting on weekend passes. Alarmed over the possible spread of social diseases, the military brass pressured city officials to shut the district down and station military police in the area.[26] While some houses closed temporarily, others continued to operate on the sly.[27]

A complete shut-down of the Beaumont district occurred for several days in the summer of 1943, after a race riot where several blacks were beaten and one was killed. In trying to restore order, Beaumont was placed under martial law. The madams and prostitutes were required to vacate their premises, and the pedestrians were restricted from the downtown streets at night.[28]

Amid the bleakness of those days, one amusing event did occur, according to a story told later to Beaumont resident Mary Ellen Wisrodt by Beaumont Police Detective Henry Austin. As a former officer who patrolled the area, Austin was shocked to find a well-known local evangelist coming out the back door of one of the "houses," his arms loaded with whiskey and fine Cuban cigars. The incident made Austin wonder, he said, just how many times the reverend had been there before.[29]

In December 1945 the American Social Hygiene Association, a national organization that monitored health conditions in houses of prostitution, issued a report to the nearby Louisiana military bases, various state and local health agencies, and the Beaumont Police Department, describing the commercialized prostitution situation in the town. Its purpose was to determine the amount and accessibility of prostitution, which might affect members of the U.S. Armed Forces and white civilians.[30]

In its survey of brothels, the American Social Hygiene Association found only three that openly conducted prostitution, two of which were considered to be cheap hotels, and one parlor house. However, it was the consensus among local cabdrivers, bellboys, bartenders, and the "man in the street," that the influx of servicemen in Beaumont would soon result in an increase in the number of brothels and other places of commercialized prostitution.[31]

Officers interviewed one prostitute who stated that she received "five dollars and up" for her services, which she considered to be "good money," especially since she had previously earned only two dollars. She attributed her good fortune to the scarcity of "hustlers" in town. Other "girls" reported that they moved to Beaumont from Galveston because of the "good business."

In addition to the investigation of brothels, the report noted that investigators questioned bellboys at various "legitimate" hotels and taverns. At one hotel a bellboy stated that "there is a girl who hustles here all the time." The officers found no evidence of pickups by clients at the hotel.. The servicemen who visited Beaumont, however, contended otherwise:

> Beaumont is a good town for us . . .
> No trouble shacking up with a girl . . .
> These girls really treat us fine . . . No,
> they are not hustlers just working
> girls and we pick them up . . .[32]

Miss Rita and other madams bided their time. They believed that the "red-light" district would soon reopen in full force. And it did.

Rita Claire Gonzales in the 1920s.
—Courtesy Papertiques of Texas.

Many photographs of this man appeared among Rita Ainsworth's collection of memorabilia.

—Courtesy Papertiques of Texas.

When Raymond Hamilton tried to hide out in one of the area brothels in the 1930s, it was reported to the Beaumont police. Officer J. O. "Fatty" Burrell went in alone to capture him.
—Courtesy R. T. Fertitta, Jr. The photo appeared in the May 1943 issue of the *Sheriffs' Association of Texas* magazine.

Rita Ainsworth in the early 1940s.
—Courtesy Papertiques of Texas

Dear Rita, I am writing something
on the back. It's a hell of a
looking will, But it's from my

CIVILIAN HOUSING BUSINESS OFFICE *heart*
EXT 2403
                                          Nat

LOCAL MAIL ADDRESS.
    YOUR NAME — *NAT-R-AINSWORTH*
    C/O. AIR DEPOT BRANCH,
    GENERAL DELIVERY,
    SPOKANE, WASH:

"To my Wife" Thurs sept 7. 1944
Dear Rita.
        In case I shouldn't come
back to you & the children, what
Property or money we should
have, Please know I want you to
do as you want to with it, Because
I know you will always care for
the children in the proper way.
            I love you always
            Nat A. Ainsworth

Copy of Nat Ainsworth's will

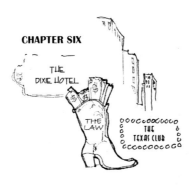

CHAPTER SIX

The 3-D Years

The post war years were prosperous times when, according to one source, the American male "discovered 3-D . . . Dacron, dandruff and dough. They found that they could wear the Dacron, get rid of the dandruff and spend the dough."[1] But, as is often true, prosperity begets promiscuity. Judging from the many stories heard on the subject, Beaumont, like the rest of the nation, was no exception. Whether it was for money or for free, the sexual revolution was in bloom, sometimes discretely, sometimes blatantly.

The following story told by Tanner Hunt illustrates one straying husband who had a not-so-clandestine rendezvous early one morning in the summer of 1954, when Hunt worked the night shift as a room clerk at the Edson Hotel after graduating from high school. Although Hunt remembered "many interesting 'goings-on' in the hotel lobby" during the wee hours, he vividly recalled the incident of the married man, who was a prominent Beaumont lawyer, walking up to the front desk with another woman and signing in under an assumed name. "They obviously had been to a party because he was wearing a tux, and she was dressed elegantly in a ball gown," Hunt said. The man paid cash in exchange for a room key, after which the couple proceeded to the elevator. "It took a minute for the elevator to get there," Hunt continued, "so all at once the woman did a handstand in the middle of the lobby, just to have something to do. Being seventeen years old, it really blew me away. I thought that was the most Fitzgerald sort of thing or a Great Gatsby sort of moment."[2]

For the free-spirited male who had money as well as passion to burn, there was an assorted list of brothels at his disposal in Beaumont. If he were new in town and didn't know his way around, he could simply look for the listing of "Jack Yule" in the local telephone directory and ask for directions. Judging from what many have said, Jack Yule really was helpful. In those days his name appeared in almost every city directory throughout the nation as the one to call.[3]

Beaumont's red-light district thrived in the years just after the war. Hotels offering services of the flesh included Rita Ainsworth's Shamrock Rooms at 250½ Bowie, the Copeland at 506½ Crockett, the Marine at 224 Tevis, and the Maryland at 388 Orange.[4] A parrot at the infamous Boston greeted patrons with "come on up, boys." He perched in the window of the hotel at 576½ Crockett Street.[5] While over at the Canary Hut on Cypress and Texas an observer might see a customer exit the place and hear him "singing just like a canary."[6]

"Miss Rita" Comes into Her Own

The boom years that followed World War II ushered in good years for both legal and illegal businesses in Jefferson County. For Rita Ainsworth, it was time to venture forward. Rita, now alienated from Nat and soon to become a widow, looked ahead to a life alone. With the expense of having his son, Charlie, in an institution, and boarding his daughter, Mary Lou, at a Catholic school, she needed a larger cash flow.[7] Soon after the war, Rita began to buy property all over town, the most notable being the Dixie Hotel on Crockett Street, which she bought on April 22, 1946, for $37,500.[8]

Within a short time, through Rita's hard work and persevering spirit, the Dixie became the finest bordello in the area. In fact, Joe Perl contended that the Dixie even might have surpassed the famed Chicken Ranch of LaGrange in notoriety.

On several occasions, Perl traveled to New York City to negotiate business contracts. One night in 1956, while staying at the

Waldorf-Astoria, he walked into the hotel's bar and was surprised to hear two men talking about his hometown. Realizing that they were traveling men, his curiosity gave way to eavesdropping when he heard one of the men say that when he traveled to Beaumont he had some good department store accounts, such as the Fair Store and the White House. "Well, forget the names of those stores," Perl recalled the other man saying. "Did you ever hear of a hotel called the Dixie?" The man answered that although he had heard about it, he had never gone there. The first man then noted to his acquaintance that if he ever went there, he could assure him that it would be an experience he'd never forget. As the man continued to rave about the Dixie, Perl couldn't remain silent any longer. He walked over to the two men and introduced himself as a resident of Beaumont. The man who had marveled so about the Dixie put his arm around him and said, "Tell him, Texas, isn't it the greatest?" Perl replied, "I can only tell you about the real estate."[9]

On another visit to New York City, friends invited Perl to a dinner where Al Jolson was performing. After the show, as an added pleasure, his friends introduced Perl to the entertainer. When Jolson heard that Joe was from Beaumont, he said, "I've heard of Beaumont. Isn't there a hotel there called the Dixie, a house of prostitution?" Joe answered by saying, "I'll tell you something, Jolie, with you singing 'Swanee' and putting the word 'Dixie' in there with such inspiration, I can see you must have been there." Jolson said that he had never been there, but he did admit that he had heard of it.[10]

An amusing story by Tanner Hunt tells about a local judge, who had traveled on business to another town and was returning by train to Beaumont. After hailing a cab, the driver asked the judge where he wanted to go. The judge mumbled, "the courthouse." Misunderstanding him and thinking he said "whorehouse," the driver drove to the Dixie. The judge had been looking at his newspaper and was surprised when the driver stopped his cab. "What are you taking me here for?" the judge asked. "I thought you wanted to go here," the driver replied. "No, I said 'courthouse,'" the judge said. "But, what the hell, as long as I'm here, I might as well pay the girls a visit." So he got out, tipped the driver, and went in.[11]

Those who recall Rita Ainsworth during the post war years

remember her as being a large, dignified woman, who was very astute in operating her businesses.[12] Soon after opening the Dixie, she endeavored to cater to the area's more elite clientele by hiring Duboise Interiors to refurbish the hotel.[13] Plush carpets were laid, rooms were painted in either pink or green with red doors, the hallway was adorned with "Gone With the Wind" movie scenes, and an expensive air-conditioning system was installed, which, according to one source, was paid for in five and ten dollar bills. The air conditioning company owner, who was unprepared to carry such a large volume of bills, was sent away with the money in a pillowcase.[14]

For many years R. T. Fertitta, Jr. operated the Elite Barber and Beauty Supply next to the Dixie Hotel. Remembering Rita and her girls well, he said that Rita was a good neighbor, and he never heard of any kind of disturbance.[15] She usually employed 10 to 12 of the prettiest girls around, most between the ages of 16 to 19, and expected them to follow her strict list of rules. They were required to have regular physical checkups, exercise daily in a small gym upstairs at the hotel, eat lunch together every day at noon, and later in the day change into evening clothes to receive their "dates."

They were mainly blondes and redheads and would often buy bleach and color for their hair at Fertitta's store. He recalled that once he was involved in a beauty show at Hotel Beaumont, which included a Clairol technician and several outstanding hairstylists. Only hours before the show began, the technician notified Fertitta of his urgent need for five or six additional girls to serve as models. He explained that once the hairstyles were completed, banners would be pinned on the girls, like in the Miss America contest, so they could parade before the audience to show off their new coiffures.

Thinking that the girls at the Dixie would welcome the opportunity to have their hair bleached and styled by the famous hairstylists, Fertittta contacted the maid at the hotel to arrange a meeting with those who might be interested in participating. When he arrived, he was ushered into a room where several girls sat. After he explained to them how fabulous they would look as models, they looked at him like he had lost his mind. "Needless to say, none of them volunteered to go," said Fertitta. "I think they thought there was something more than just using them as models."[16]

At the Dixie, Miss Rita received guests on the second floor, but only after they passed inspection. She used a peephole in the door at the top of the stairs through which she surveyed potential guests. Once inside, they might have a drink at the bar before going to one of the parlors where several women would appear. After the client had chosen his date, a buzzer was pushed to signal the maid. The maid would push a switch to lock all other doors leading into the hallway. The man followed his date down the hall to a bedroom and other guests did not see them. Once inside, the maid locked the room, and, to further maintain the client's anonymity, she kept it locked until the girl signaled her. She sounded another buzzer to clear the hallway until the patron was safely out of sight and thus preserved his anonymity by avoiding any embarrassing meetings among men who did not want to be seen.[17]

Joe Perl recalled that Rita occasionally closed the hotel for private parties given by prominent businessmen, who would pay up to $2,500 for the night, which was considered an expensive fee in those days. As a friend, Rita once invited Joe to view the place before a party began. "I couldn't believe how lavish it looked," he said. "She had flowers everywhere. She had two bartenders and three other people to help serve the food, champagne, and mixed drinks." Rita and Perl went into the kitchen, and she proudly displayed beautifully decorated plates of food that she had ordered from Houston. "I remember her saying that anybody who wanted to be with one of her girls would have to pay $50," Perl continued. "I can assure you that in those days no one needed Viagra.[18]

In addition to closing the Dixie for the swinging local "blue bloods," Rita sometimes hosted parties for her good friend Sheriff Charley Meyer when he wanted to entertain sheriffs from other counties. "His deputies were the rag men," said Meyer's successor, former Sheriff R. E. "Dick" Culbertson. "They would have towels on their arms, and whenever one of the guests had too much to drink, it was their job to clean them up."[19]

A popular story depicting the close ties between Ainsworth and Meyer took place one year when the local A&M chapter held its annual fund-raising party at the Harvest Club. The Aggies sold tickets to a car raffle, their main moneymaker, and they sold a multitude of tickets. The winning ticket received the grand prize, and the person who sold it also received a prize, so sellers wrote their names on every ticket they sold. The crowd that night could hardly believe it when the announcer called Rita Ainsworth's name. She held the winning ticket, and the name written on the ticket was Charley Meyer. From then on, many people began referring to the A&M Club as the Ainsworth and Meyer Club.[20] Rita, a charitable lady, put the car to good use. She loaned it to a local Alcoholics Anonymous chapter that was making monthly trips to Huntsville to form a chapter for prisoners.[21]

Members of the local AA chapter acknowledged Rita's generous nature, as did members of other local organizations. When the Optimist Club organized the first Little League baseball system in Beaumont, Rita willingly agreed to sponsor a team. Later when it came time to advertise the sponsors, Little League officials decided that it would be in the best interest of everyone concerned to have her remain an anonymous donor.[22]

A devout Catholic, Rita once assisted a church of another denomination in its building project. When the founders of the church planned a reception to consecrate the church, Rita loaned them her sterling silver punch bowl with matching cups that normally sat on a piano in one of her parlors. Although she overwhelmed the founders with her generosity, they wondered how many of their parishioners might think the bowl looked familiar.[23]

During the 1950s, the Dixie Hotel was often referred to as the "Beaumont Club Annex" since some members of the club, which was located on the 6th floor of the Edson Hotel on Liberty Street, could exit into the alleyway. They used a covered stairway that led to the back door of the Dixie.[24] Many longtime residents believed that Rita constructed the cover mainly to protect the anonymity of the guests visiting from the Beaumont Club. But Rita's stepdaughter, Mary Lou, maintained that the canopy originated for another reason, which she relates from a story told to her by Rita:

> One night, always in the dark, a [prominent] gentleman caller visited the Dixie. He went down the back stairs, slick and wet, as there was a rainstorm that night. The gentleman slipped on the stairs and fell halfway down into the alley below and broke his leg. The maid, Mis' "Lilly Belle," called Mis' Rita. Mother went down and saw what happened. She called for an ambulance . . .

So he was taken away. Then a month later Mother put up the cover over the stairs, so that no one would get hurt again.

We would laugh and laugh over this story [about the canopy being built to protect the anonymity of visitors]. It has been told falsely in more than one newspaper article.[25]

Being a "high class" place, the Dixie did not cater to the local youths, especially to those who didn't have money to spend. One man recalled that when he was a teenager, Miss Rita occasionally permitted him and some of his friends into one of the parlors in the early evening to play a pinball machine before the customers arrived. "Many times the girls would be sitting around, so we could flirt with them, pat them on the rear, and, if we were lucky, get a good feel," he said. "George Jones [the country and western singer] would sometimes tag along. He lived in Vidor then, but on Saturday nights he'd come to town and play his guitar and sing for tips while sitting on a curb nearby."[26]

Apparently, the teenager felt so comfortable with the surroundings at the Dixie that he decided to get a job so he could do more than just play a pinball machine. He became a paying customer instead. He joined the Pipe Fitters Union, whose union hall was next door to the Dixie, separated only by a fire door. Although the youth admitted visiting other area establishments, he remembered Rita's as the best place to go.[27]

As a customer at the Dixie, the man learned that Rita, like many of the other madams in the area, was a member of a "circuit," which rotated girls from one brothel to another. "Her circuit included Lake Charles, Lafayette, and Opelousas," the man said. "The girls weren't dumb, but they weren't high IQ operators either. They were just pretty girls who probably had the opportunity to get out of the Bayou Country and figured they had something that would give them an income."[28]

Besides the "circuit" girls, Tanner Hunt remembered that one summer when he was a student in college, it was rumored that Rita had hired a Theta from SMU, who was trying to earn a little extra money for college. "Everyone was telling everyone else about the wonderful summer addition," he said. "According to the boys who patronized the place, she was certainly attractive and well-spoken enough to be a Theta. Whether it was true or not, it certainly did a lot to improve Rita's income that summer."[29]

In the late '50s, the Internal Revenue Service became more stringent in its examination of income tax returns, particularly of businesses where profits were high. One year, the IRS questioned Rita about the large deductions she claimed for the institutional care of her stepson, Charlie. Not satisfied with her answers, the agency stationed an employee at the Dixie. He counted the towels used each day by the Dixie as an efficient way to establish her true income. At any rate, the agent seemed to enjoy his job so much that one day Rita had enough and ordered him off her premises.[30]

Like many other "house" operators, Rita expected her girls to take the required precautions, yet sometimes a girl became pregnant, nevertheless. Rita recognized that pregnancy simply was one of the hazards of the trade. Did she hire a Beaumont doctor, a known abortionist, to terminate unexpected pregnancies? No one can answer that question with absolute certainty. Dale Sheffield of Lumberton recalled that Rita took good care of the girls in the advanced stages of pregnancy. In the late 1940s, Sheffield and her sister rented a duplex from Rita on Tyrrell Street in Beaumont. Next door, one of Rita's girls stayed for about four months until she had her baby. "We never saw her in anything but a negligee. If the girl needed anything, a cab brought it," Dale said. "I was kind of a snob back then, but my sister would sometimes take her to a drive-in movie at night. When the baby was born, we never saw her again."[31]

Rita Ainsworth lived a life outside the social mores of society, but except for that, she exhibited many of the characteristics one finds in outstanding citizens in the community—charitable, supportive, and concerned for those who depended upon her for their welfare.

The Loss of Innocence

In the 1950s some of the more prominent fathers in Beaumont still adhered to the archaic belief that when a son reached puberty it was the father's duty to enroll him in a sex education class. A father often found such a class at a local house of prostitution. After all, proper young men should leave the "nice" girls alone.[32]

One local man remembered his father taking him to the Dixie to "look around" when he was 15 years old. However, since the minimum age of patronization at the Dixie was 16, he took his money as well as his passion down the street to the Boston Hotel, where the madam was more sympathetic to the needs of the more youthful patrons.

He had finished his first year at Allen Academy in Bryan and was home for the summer when his father gave him $50 to spend. After he arrived at the hotel, a hostess invited him into the parlor and introduced him to three or four girls. He recalled that his selection was a blonde, who wore an Arabian outfit with "see-through" leg parts. When he inquired about the price, the girl said that it depended on what he wanted. Being inexperienced and only 15, he asked her what she meant. "Well, you can get a 'straight' for $15, or you can get a 'half-and-half' for $25," the girl answered. "It's called 'around the world.'" Since he had the money, he answered, "I'll take the works. . . ." After the works, he later said, "I felt I had been around the world in 30 minutes."[33]

The Marine Hotel on Tevis was even more lax with its minimum age requirements, and reportedly even solicited the younger men. John Parsons, a member of the Special Services Vice Squad of the Beaumont Police Department, stated that during the vice squad's investigation, he questioned Annabelle, one of the maids at the Marine, about the ages of the youthful customers. He was shocked when he learned that the hotel manager reserved the hotel on Sunday afternoons for the younger boys, many of whom were 14 years old and younger. Annabelle indicated that the boys often saved their lunch money to afford the visit. Parsons stated, "She was so honest, you couldn't doubt her."[34] Other sources indicate that the Maryland Hotel provided a special service for those who had recently "come of age" by offering an introductory lesson for a mere $5.[35] One young man fell deeply in love with his teacher during his first visit. He remembered her as "a beautiful, movie-star blonde," who was very thoughtful and kind. "I remember laying on her bed afterwards watching her brush her hair," he said.

He visited the Maryland several times after that night and always wanted a "date" with her. One night as he pulled up before the hotel, he noticed an older man stepping out of a fancy Cadillac. He followed the man into the parlor. Once inside, he saw his teacher waiting for the man at the top of the stairs. "I'll never forget how I felt watching him follow her into her room. I was consumed with jealousy. Years later, I saw her obituary. She had been killed in a car accident."[36]

The 3-D years touched young men in various ways. Where one eagerly "spent the dough" for pleasure and enlightenment, the next one observed the scene only vicariously and "saved his dough." Although World War II had ended the Depression, prosperity powered new social attitudes, both positive and negative. Yet all the while, the madams in the bordellos found new approaches to educate the young and to gratify the old. Prostitution continued to flourish in Jefferson County.

Some people never know when they've got enough!

Art that was featured on the back side of the Dixie Hotel's business cards.
—Courtesy, *The Examiner*, June 20, 2001

Officers of the 1950 Beaumont Police Department, along with "Johnnie," the mascot of the Phillip Morris Tobacco Company. Police Chief Jim Mulligan is shown standing fourth from right, front row. Assistant Chief of Police Clyde Rush is second from right, front row.

—Courtesy James C. Rush

Early black officers of the Beaumont Police Department, circa 1954. Pictured left to right: Phillip Millaton, Buster Turner, Jr., Earl Bill, Eddie Cole.

—Courtesy Buster Turner, Jr.

Crockett Street in downtown Beaumont in the early 1950s.
—Courtesy the Tyrrell Historical Library

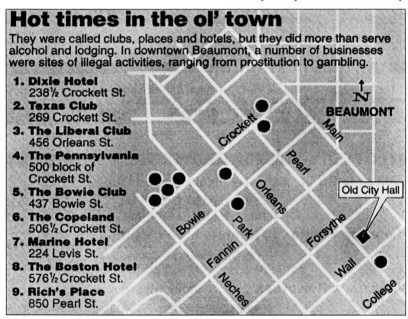

Hot times in the ol' town

They were called clubs, places and hotels, but they did more than serve alcohol and lodging. In downtown Beaumont, a number of businesses were sites of illegal activities, ranging from prostitution to gambling.

1. **Dixie Hotel**
   238½ Crockett St.
2. **Texas Club**
   269 Crockett St.
3. **The Liberal Club**
   456 Orleans St.
4. **The Pennsylvania**
   500 block of
   Crockett St.
5. **The Bowie Club**
   437 Bowie St.
6. **The Copeland**
   506½ Crockett St.
7. **Marine Hotel**
   224 Levis St.
8. **The Boston Hotel**
   576½ Crockett St.
9. **Rich's Place**
   850 Pearl St.

N

BEAUMONT

Old City Hall

Map showing the sites of some of the early businesses involved in illegal activities in downtown Beaumont.
—Microfilm photo from the *Beaumont Enterprise.*
Courtesy the Beaumont Public Library

The above pictures reflect a coin found in the remodeling of the Boston Hotel for occupancy of the Moore, Landrey Law Firm on Crockett Street in Beaumont. Just how the coin arrived there is left to one's imagination.

—Courtesy Floyd A. Landrey

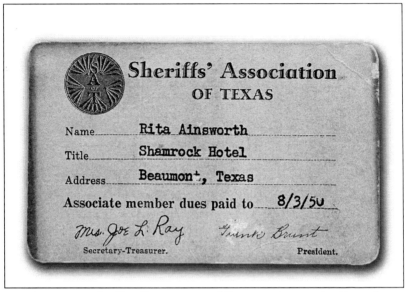

Rita Ainsworth's Sheriffs' Association of Texas associate membership card.
—Courtesy Papertiques of Texas

Drawing from the June 1962 issue of the Cavalier Magazine

Drawing from the June 1962 issue of Cavalier Magazine

Girls dressed for the evening at the Dixie
—Courtesy Crockett Street Entertainment District

Birthday celebration at the Dixie Hotel. According to historians at the Tyrrell Historical Library, the young woman sitting next to Rita Ainsworth, far right, is throught to be her step-daughter, who lived and attended school at a convent. The other two women possibly worked for Rita.

—The William H. McCain collection, file 1,
Courtesy the Tyrrell Historical Library

Rita Ainsworth in the 1950s.
—Microfilm photo from the *Beaumont Enterprise.*
Courtesy the Beaumont Public Library

CHAPTER SEVEN

The Numbers Game

Choose your numbers! Give me the odds! Place your bets! Lay it down! One always could find a game in town. There was no doubt that by the 1930s, '40s and '50s the downtown area in Beaumont was hopping with seamy gambling establishments. Russell L. Bond must have realized that the town was a fertile field in which to set up his illegal game of chance, because he moved to Beaumont in 1938 to establish what was to become one of the chief gambling operations in the area, the numbers racket. In 1940, Bond became partners with Jerome A. "Jake" Giles, Jr., a member of a well-known Beaumont family and a reputed local racketeer.[1] The partnership would become a union Bond would live to regret.

He established outlets for the game in many barber shops and small grocery stores throughout the area.[2] Also, there were various "policy" houses within the black communities, so named because players often used money to bet on the numbers rather than pay on their insurance policies.[3]

The mechanics of the game mirrored, on a more informal basis, our modern-day lottery system: there was a morning draw and an afternoon draw. A player would pick his numbers and give his money to a "writer," who would write down the bets and give a copy to the player. After holding out 20 percent for his services, the writer would put 80 percent of the original bet in an envelope and place it in a bag. A runner would pick up the bag and deliver the bag to headquarters, where the numbers were drawn. The runner would then return to each writer his envelopes with the slips, designating the winning numbers.[4]

According to Tanner Hunt, the headquarters of the numbers racket in Beaumont was a small wooden structure in Jake Giles' back yard. It was there that the runners, who were mainly blacks, brought their day's proceeds and picked up the money to pay off the winning numbers. "They were always to call out from a distance and then wait until they were told to come forward," said Hunt. "If you stepped on that porch, it was death. This was the fear he [Giles] had engendered in these people."[5]

The numbers game became so profitable that in 1949, Giles decided to reduce taxes by making partners of employees H. R. Calendar and D. L. Evans, Jr. Russell Bond contended that he quit the rackets in disgust in 1957, when Giles and his cohorts wanted to start rigging the numbers and cheating the players for a larger house gain. The game was illegal, yet Bond insisted that they had to run it honestly to keep the players coming.[6]

Giles continued to oversee the operation until July 3, 1958, when he was shot and killed by Lee Wesley "Banjo Red" Marshall in the 200 block of Crockett Street.[7] As to the motive for the killing, longtime residents have offered numerous theories, some almost too incredible to believe. While one source contends that the shooting resulted from simply an argument between the pair, other versions offer a more sinister explanation, saying that Marshall was the "hit" man for the Mafia, hired to eliminate Giles after he refused to allow the notorious criminal organization in on the action.

Jerry Conn, who worked at the *Beaumont Enterprise* during the summer after his sophomore year at the University of Texas, recalled accompanying *Enterprise* photographer Elmer Trumble to the murder scene of Jake Giles. They arrived to see the ambulance personnel loading the body of Giles into the back of an ambulance, and both men noticed Banjo Red seated in a patrol car. They followed the patrol car to the police station where the officers led Marshall to the booking desk. Conn remembered Banjo Red as a big, sloppy-looking guy wearing a Panama hat. As he leaned over the booking desk, a police officer asked him, "Banjo Red, did you shoot Jake Giles?" Marshall answered, "Yeah, I shot the son-of-a-bitch, and I'm glad I did it."[8]

A Jefferson County grand jury indicted Marshall on September 11, 1958. He was tried and a jury found him guilty without malice. On January 24, 1959, he was sentenced to two years in the state penitentiary. Marshall's lawyer appealed and the guilty verdict was reversed.[9] On the re-trial of the case, a jury acquitted Marshall on October 14, 1964. Members of the jury determined that Marshall acted in self-defense after hearing his testimony that Giles had threatened him and slapped him twice.[10]

Marshall testified at his second trial that he and Giles previously had been friends. Their friendship waned, however, after Marshall, who was a pipe fitter, repeatedly refused to become a partner in the numbers racket. He stated that Giles believed if Marshall could get the pipe fitters to play the numbers, it would increase the gross of the racket by $1 million to $2 million a year.[11]

Before Jake Giles met his violent death, his family had faced two previous tragic events in their lives. In 1916, Jerome "Jake" Giles, Sr., a Jefferson County sheriff, who was reported to be one of the most popular peace officers in the state, was shot and killed by Ida Hadley, the wife of Paul Hadley, a fugitive who faced charges of assault in Jefferson County and who had fled with Ida to Kansas City. After local officers apprehended the pair, Giles traveled to Kansas City to return them to Beaumont. On the train ride back, Ida shot Giles as he slept.[12]

Tragedy faced the family again 25 years later, this time not at the hands of an outsider, but within the family itself. On July 25, 1942, Jake, Jr., shot and killed his brother Robert Barber "Bob" Giles on Crockett Street in Beaumont after an argument between the two in Fuller's Bar. At the time of the unfortunate incident, both men, former police officers, were employed at Magnolia Refinery in Beaumont.[13]

The shooting of the 36-year-old Bob Giles appalled the southeast Texas community. Citizens had regarded him as a highly respected Beaumont police sergeant, as well as an outstanding athlete and scholar in high school and college. Equally outstanding in his youth, Jake was cited during World War I for bravery in saving a fellow sailor's life during an explosion aboard a warship.

After Jake killed his brother, he was released on $2,000 bail and tried for murder in the Jefferson County Criminal District Court the following September. He pleaded not guilty, saying the killing was committed in self-defense; the jurors must have believed him, for on September 30, they returned a verdict of "not guilty."[14]

In spite of Giles' propensity toward violence, he, like the "Godfather," sought solace in his garden. Longtime horticulturists still credit Jake and his wife for introducing rare varieties of camellias into the southeast Texas area.[15]

Mr. and Mrs. Jake Giles, pictured in their garden in 1955.
—Courtesy V. J. Barranco

Site where local racketeer Jerome A. "Jake" Giles was killed on July 3, 1958 in the 200 block of Crockett Street in Beaumont.
—Microfilm photo from the *Beaumont Enterprise.*
Courtesy the Beaumont Public Library

Lee Wesley "Banjo Red" Marshall as he was booked at the Beaumont Police Department on July 3, 1958, following the shooting death of Jerome A. "Jake" Giles.
—Microfilm photo from the *Beaumont Enterprise.*
Courtesy the Beaumont Public Library

Jerome A. "Jake" Giles, far right front row, served on the 1913 Beaumont High Shcool football team. Owen Lord, who later became a judge of the Jefferson County Criminal District Court, is pictured second from right, top row.

—Courtesy Central High School

Robert Barber "Bob" Giles as he was pictured in the 1925 Beaumont High School yearbook.
—Courtesy Central High School

CHAPTER EIGHT

"Blue Buddy" Was "The Man"

The strict division of racial groups prior to the desegregation movement in the mid-1950s created out of necessity a bustling entertainment network that catered mainly to the African-American communities in Jefferson County. While the western area of Port Arthur around West 7th Street and Grannis Avenue teemed with blacks enjoying the nightlife, nothing could compare to the lively black communities in Beaumont, especially along Irving Street, where there were approximately 23 or 24 beer taverns. Gilbert Alex, the present owner of Club Signature on Irving, recalled that during the post war period Irving Street bustled with so much activity that it resembled Bourbon Street in New Orleans.[1]

Besides the taverns, other establishments provided lively entertainment in the black community. Cheney's Auditorium featured live entertainment. Gilbert's Hotel rented upstair rooms by the week and downstair rooms by the hour. The popular Raven on the corner of Irving and Grand, owned by M. C. "Blue Buddy" Carter, the best known and most flamboyant African-American entrepreneur of his time, brought in nationally known entertainers.[2]

Nicknamed "Blue Buddy" as a child by his friends, who said he was so black he was almost blue, Carter opened the Raven on November 1, 1948. He soon started booking shows out of California and New York, featuring such notable black performers as Ray

Charles, Sam Cooke, Bobby "Blue" Bland, B. B. King, Dinah Washington, and Ike and Tina Turner. Nat "King" Cole and others who performed at the Harvest Club or the City Auditorium also gathered at the Raven to "have a party" after their shows. Despite the popularity of such stars, most hotels would not cater to African Americans. So it was Carter's job to arrange for their suitable accommodations.[3]

Next door to the Raven, Carter built an oyster bar, which he later converted into the Blue Note Club.[4] Behind the clubs, he built a gambling shack. His close ties to Jake Giles and Beaumont police officials, who considered him one of their best informants, enabled him to be the only black operator to sell liquor by the drink and operate a gambling establishment.[5]

Gabe Duriso, a former waiter at the Raven, remembered the time when the Birdland, named after a club in New York, opened, and the crowd went there instead of to the Raven. "Soon it was closed," said Duriso, "because 'Blue' was 'the man.'" While working at the Raven, Duriso remembered that Liquor Control Board supervisor El Roy Mauldin would raid the club from time to time and confiscate the liquor. "We didn't believe it, but the same trucks that loaded it up and hauled it away were the same trucks that brought it back about an hour or two later," he said. "Curtis Booker, who was Blue's right-hand man, would say, 'What are you taking it for? You know you're going to have to bring it back.'"[6]

Gene Corder was a rookie patrolman on the Beaumont police force and quickly came to understand the power of Blue Buddy's immunity from the law. After giving Carter a ticket for going 50 miles per hour in a 30-mile zone, fellow patrolman Gene Carpenter asked him who had received the ticket. Corder answered, "A guy by the name of M. C. Carter, who was just flying down Main Street here." Carpenter explained to Corder the special relationship Carter enjoyed with the local law officials and said that the ticket would be quickly voided. "Sure enough, when I walked into the station, the captain had already gotten a call and told me to give him all the copies of the ticket," said Corder. "When I asked why, he answered, 'Don't ask questions, boy. Give me the ticket.' I never forgot it."[7]

Reverend G. W. Daniels, pastor of the Starlight Baptist Church in Beaumont, remembered "Blue Buddy" in his youth as "a very handsome boy who came from Louisiana after the death of his mother to live with his aunt and uncle, Reverend and Mrs. S. I. Mitchell. However," Daniels said, "when he got out of school, he went the other way. He was sort of a 'Casanova' boy. His aunt and uncle were really hurt over it."[8]

No one knows what influences changed Blue Buddy from a "God-fearing Baptist" to the "wheeler-dealer" of the African-American community. He developed a friendship with Bob Giles, whom he met while working as a youth at Hotel Beaumont, and it may have been a contributing factor. Bob Giles introduced Blue Buddy to his infamous brother, Jake, and from then on, Blue Buddy became the proverbial entrepreneur, operating the Carter Cleaners, a drugstore, an ice cream parlor, and a gambling shack on the north end of Gladys Street before building Club Raven. Those who knew him remembered that he always drove the finest of cars, wore flashy jewelry, owned a multitude of dress suits and wore Edwin Clapp fashion shoes. "Blue Buddy was Jake's boy," said Buster Turner. "And as long as he stayed in line, he did good."[9]

Following the vice raids of December 3, Blue Buddy appeared before the House Committee on New Year's Day, 1961. When questioned about the activities at his businesses, he admitted that "they shot a little dice" and played a little game called "Georgia Skin." He attributed his good fortune in never being arrested to "Lady Luck," but his income tax return, which earlier had been subpoenaed by the committee, revealed that this so-called "luck" may have been the result of his yearly payment of $1,850 for "police protection."[10]

Carter's attorney advised him to leave town during the televised public hearings, thinking Carter might divulge too much information to the investigators. Instead of going elsewhere, however, he traveled to the county jail for safekeeping, where Sheriff Meyer arranged for him to have the best of care. When Tom James learned that Blue Buddy was a no-show, he jokingly called out to the delight of everyone, "Won't you please come back, Blue Buddy, wherever you are?"[11]

Soon after the public hearings, Blue Buddy, like some of the other vice operators, attempted to go back into gambling surreptitiously. But it didn't take long under the new circumstances for him to decide that gambling just wasn't worth the gamble. From then on, he focused his attention on booking entertainers at the Raven. When the club burned in 1966, he began organizing dances at the Beaumont Sportatorium and working with the Neches YMCA committee to bring in such popular performers as the Mills Brothers.[12] Finally, in his later years and in poor health, he returned to his religious roots, serving as an usher at the Scott Olive Baptist Church, where his uncle had preached for many years.[13]

In spite of his worldly ways, Blue Buddy will long be remembered as one of the most likeable and colorful personalities in the black community, a man who probably employed more blacks than any other businessman in the area, all at a time when life was anything but easy.

YOU ARE INVITED TO MINGLE WITH THE CROWD
THAT WILL CELEBRATE THE OPENING OF

"THE RAVEN"

BEAUMONT'S NEWEST NIGHT SPOT MON. NIGHT, NOV. 1, 1948

Corner of Grant and Irving Streets

Music by

JAMES LEE AND HIS ORCHESTRA

WITH STAR STUDDED ATTRACTIONS

M. C. by Leo Simmon

Station K. T. R. M. Will Make a Broadcast, From the Raven

Don't Miss It

FIRST FLOOR SHOW 10:00 O'Clock   SECOND 12:00 O'Clock

CURTIS BOOKER, Manager
M. C. CARTER, Owner

Invitation announcing the opening of the Raven.

—Courtesy Roy Dunn

Partying at the Raven. Seated, left to right: Frank Patillo, Jr., Alice Patillo, Alice Pantantion, L. C. Pantantion.

—Courtesy Frank Patillo, III

M. C. "Blue Buddy" Carter
—The Penny Clark
collection, Box 1, File 1.
Courtesy the Tyrrell
Historical Library

Members of the Appomattox Club, circa 1958. Left to right, seated: Dr. C. H. D. Fleming, Stanford Prater, Terry Cooper, Prentice Adams. Standing: M. C. Carter, Charles Rosenthal, Mitchell Norman, Ben Willis, Joe Parker, Laverne Smith.
—Courtesy Chuck Guillory

CHAPTER NINE

Tales from South Jefferson County

While "Miss Rita," Jake Giles, and the club operators on Crockett Street were busy honing their skills in Beaumont, south Jefferson County was also establishing itself as a seedy haven for illegal operations. One Beaumont patrolman remembered on his first trip south that he was told by a superior officer to "take a deep breath of fresh air; we're about to make a transition. We're about to enter Port Arthur."[1]

Roy Dunn, the owner of the weekly newspaper *The Penny Record* in Bridge City, recalled that his father, Clay Dunn, was a creative innovator who looked for about any opportunity, whether legal or illegal, to make a good living. Establishing the first taxi service in Port Arthur, Clay soon earned enough cash in 1928 to build the Silver Slipper on Lake Street in Bridge City, one of the first supper clubs in the area. "Many prominent people patronized the place because there was gambling and alcoholic drinks," said Roy. "He also put in the first liquor store in Orange County and had a ship built to bootleg whiskey from Nassau." The Ku Klux Klan looked unkindly toward Clay's illegal money-making endeavors during the Prohibition years, so, one night someone tarred and feathered him in the Port Acres vicinity. "He hid out for about six months at the home of an elderly Cajun couple," remembered Roy. "In appreciation, he bought them a home." Not a person to be discouraged, Clay later started a business called the "Ponies of America" in the area where he and his brothers raised and sold Appaloosa horses and eventually bought property, which he called the Avalon Ranch in Burleson County between Bryan and Caldwell.[2]

After Clay's death, Roy inherited the Avalon Ranch and years later built a club on the property called the Trade Winds in Bryan, on the Brazos River. "There were striptease girls, bands, and Las Vegas acts," said Roy. He also admitted to having owned the first liquor store in Brazos County after the county voted "wet." Since many citizens were opposed to the new ordinance and refused to sell their land for a liquor store, Roy decided to find out what lands in the county were available to him. He soon discovered that one of the cemeteries in the county had never been set aside as a public domain, so he built his store in the middle of the cemetery. "People shot at me during the night and went to the judge to try to get me out," Roy said. Fortunately for him, the law, as well as the judge, was on his side. "The judge told them that there were two things they could do," Roy continued. "They could either sell it or they could divide it. Since they couldn't sell the dead or divide it, there was nothing they could do."

When the vice investigation heated up in Jefferson County in the late '50s, Roy indicated he was "scared to death they were going to get us. In fact, Joe Teague, who was my father's good friend and known as the bagman in Port Arthur, the man who collected the payoff money from the "houses" and the gamblers, hid out at one of my ranch houses until everything cooled off."[3]

D. P. Moore, an early Port Arthur policeman who later became assistant chief of police in Port Arthur, recalled the days when he "walked the beat" on Houston Avenue in the seedier part of town. "Most of the prostitutes in Port Arthur had pimps," he said. "Generally each pimp had four or five girls. They wore fine clothes, which, of course, the girls paid for."[4]

Judging from a story told to Liz Hanna by her father, Grover Shifflett, an employee of Gulf Oil, the "girls" and their procurers felt free to solicit business at the docks and gates of the Gulf Oil and Texaco refineries in Port Arthur. "They would greet the seamen coming off the ships and the local workers during a shift change," Hanna said. "The pimps would gladly provide free rides to the 'houses,' and the girls often would pass out business cards offering free drinks."[5]

Native Port Arthurian Oliver "Sonny" Lawson, who worked one summer between his junior and senior years in high school at the Port Arthur Menhaden Fishery, recalled the blatant solicitation of the menhaden "pogy" fishermen. "When the boats docked, the place swarmed with prostitutes and pimps, waiting for the guys to clean up under the big outside shower. The guys would be so eager that 3 or 4 of them would shower together. Then they'd jump in one of the cars and be whisked away."[6]

The illicit dandies may have felt safe in gathering on the docks of the refineries and fishery, but they were careful not to loiter on the streets of Port Arthur. Too often the police arrested them and carried them off to jail. "And if they protested in any way," said one man, "they were beaten up and dumped out on the other side of the Rainbow Bridge in Orange County."[7]

When asked to describe a few of the houses of prostitution in Port Arthur, D. P. Moore recalled: "The L&M was a flop house where winos frequented. . . . The Paradise Hotel was run by a black man by the name of Hannah. . . . Betty's Place was run by a large woman who didn't put up with any rowdiness. One night a bunch of seamen started a fight, and she whipped them all and threw them out the door."[8]

The Green House was another well-known Port Arthur brothel, remembered by many locals as the place that almost went up in flames one night when a group of more-than-mischievous teenage boys decided to go on a rampage. Believing it would be great fun to cause a commotion at a house of prostitution, the pranksters bought a gallon of gasoline, drove up to the Green House, and threw the gas onto the front porch. As one boy ignited it, another rang the doorbell, and then they all quickly sped away. Fortunately, the fire department quickly extinguished the blaze, and all the inhabitants in the house bailed out the windows before anyone was hurt. The police arrested the perpetrators later that night for starting a fight with a foreign seaman. Soon after their arrival at the police station, one of the boys spotted their empty gasoline can and immediately admitted their involvement in the earlier offense. The police officers recognized their guilt and told them that their malicious actions would surely result in prison sentences. The officers locked the boys in a cell for an overnight stay. The boys were released the next morning after their fathers paid substantial fines.[9]

"When in Port Arthur, Visit Grace Woodyard's"

Of the 14 known brothels in town, locals described Grace Woodyard's as one of the most successful enterprises around, mostly because of the patronage of the many visiting seamen. In fact, seafarers circulated a legend about the notoriety of the place that involved a group of sailors who scrawled a message onto the hull of their overturned ship off the African Coast. As they clung to their ship they wrote "When in Port Arthur, visit Grace Woodyard's."[10]

Hilda Vickers, who worked at Lipoff's Jewelry Store on Proctor Street for 16 years, remembered Woodyard as a regular customer. "When she came into our store," said Vickers, "she always looked a sight with her orange, unruly hair."

She was married to a bootlegger named Rusty Woodyard. The two illegal entrepreneurs made so much money that they were able to afford a maid to care for their two children in a very nice house in a fashionable residential neighborhood. Their son, Jimmie, was very likable, and when he was a senior in high school in 1939, he was voted king of his class. The mother of the queen was furious when she found out that a madam's son was to escort her daughter to the dance.[11]

The stories told about Woodyard by Vickers and others were just about as wild and colorful as her hair. It's said the seamen who hung out at her place had so much fun that they would often spend all their money and wake up without a dime. But, to make them feel better, she'd give them enough to get back to their ship. Vickers also remembered two sisters who worked alternate shifts. "One was a mother and the wife of a man who shipped out," said Vickers. "To make ends meet while he was away, she would work, and her sister stayed home with her children."[12]

The desires of the flesh enabled Woodyard to survive the days of the Great Depression while still maintaining her charitable nature. One year when the officials of the city of Port Arthur couldn't pay the electric bill, she volunteered to pay it for them. However, as solvent as her business remained, she was ever-aware of the economic forces at play. Once when she was walking down a sidewalk on Proctor Street, she met a car dealer and began visiting with him about their financial hardships. "It's really been tough," the car dealer said. "If I don't sell some cars, I'm going to lose my ass." Woodyard nodded her head in agreement. "Yeah, I know what you mean," she answered. "If I don't sell some ass, I'm going to lose my cars."[13]

Like many other illegal operators in the town, she was in close alliance with the local police, whom she never hesitated to call when she foresaw trouble. One man vividly recalled the time he and his friends celebrated at Grace Woodyard's soon after their return from the Korean conflict. It was a wild evening, especially when one of his buddies caused a rift by refusing to put on his clothes and leave. "He was a crazy paratrooper who got high on beer and didn't want to get out of bed," the man said. "He just laughed and giggled and wouldn't get up. But when Gracie threatened to call the cops, we went up there and finally got him to put his clothes on and get out of there."[14]

Tragedy struck the Woodyard family on July 26, 1959 when Jimmie's wife, Sydna Woodyard, was killed in a horse related accident. With young children to raise and the demanding business of operating the Silver Saddle Motel in North Hollywood, California, Jimmie called for his mother's help. Grace traveled extensively between Texas and California until her business was shut down in Port Arthur following the vice probe. Rusty died several months later, and Grace moved permanently to California, where she lived until her death on February 2, 1979.[15]

Marcella's

Grace Woodyard may have operated one of the most financially successful brothels in town, but Marcella Chadwell was perhaps the most beloved madam, remembered by many for her generosity and charm. According to an article written by Tim Knight in the *Port Arthur Centennial History 1898-1998* and several newspaper articles, Marcella was born in New Orleans on December 12, 1894, and moved to Port Arthur around the turn of the century to live with an aunt after her father was killed in a railroad accident. Known as a free spirit even in her youth, she visited a tattoo parlor one day and had a rose tattooed onto her upper right arm.

She married young, but became a widow with a son to support after her husband, Herman Irving, died in the 1918 influenza epidemic. In the early 1920s, Marcella went to work as a sales girl in downtown Port Arthur at Deutser Brothers Dry Goods Store. While there, she began to notice a group of young women who came into the store once a month to order fine clothing from New York catalogs. One day she was especially impressed when a stately, well-dressed woman left the store and stepped into a chauffeured, very fine Pierce-Arrow automobile with a sign on its back bumper that read, "Get like me." When she learned that the mysterious woman was a madam who operated a rooming house that entertained men for money, she decided that she wanted to wear nice clothes and ride around in a limousine, too. So she hired two young girls, quit her job at Deutser's, and watched her business grow.

Soon after, Marcella married a bootlegger named Guy Chadwell. But, unfortunately, she became a widow again when Guy died violently at the hands of the Port Arthur police on August 10, 1925. According to local lore, Chadwell was shot and killed by Port Arthur Police Chief H. F. Baker after he was arrested for bootlegging and refused to be escorted in a paddy wagon to the police station because a black man was inside the wagon.[16]

Marcella faced more heartache when her son, Emmett, developed a muscular disease that confined him to a wheelchair and eventually killed him. She later developed a relationship with a much younger man by the name of Claude Rambeau, who fancied himself her business agent and was often seen driving around town in a convertible. In 1941, they bought a house at 328 Fifth Street in Port Arthur, which served as both their home and Marcella's business. At various times, her girls also operated from the Melba Hotel at 344½ Proctor Street and from the Villa Hotel at 124½ Sixth Street.[17]

Like many brothels in the area, Marcella's hotels were good places for men to go for mixed drinks. Port Arthur resident Joe Hughes recalled that as a young man, he and his friends often congregated for drinks at Marcella's Fifth Street location. "I soon became acquainted with her and once or twice attended a private dinner party in her quarters upstairs," Joe said.[18]

When Texas state law enforcement officers shut down the illegal businesses in Jefferson County and the legislative committee issued subpoenas for the vice operators to appear at the January, 1961, public hearings, Marcella, like many others, left the area. Marcella fled to a place on the Sabine River to avoid being summoned. One evening, Hughes and some of his friends decided to pay her a visit. "While we were watching 'Wanted: Dead or Alive,' starring Steve McQueen, on TV," he said "we could hardly believe it when Marcella told us that McQueen once worked at her place."[19]

Although Hughes never doubted Marcella at the time, her comment concerning McQueen gained even more merit when he later read *Steve McQueen, Portrait of an American Rebel* by Marshall Terrill. In the book, McQueen readily admitted being employed as a towel boy at a brothel in the Dominican Republic and living in Port Arthur, Texas, before taking acting lessons in New York City.[20]

As time went on, Claude Rambeau left Marcella, married another woman, and moved to Las Vegas. He eventually returned, however, and continued to live with Marcella until her death in 1989.[21]

Savannah's

Savannah Godeaux joined the group of established madams in Port Arthur in 1949, when she opened what was to become the well-known African-American hotel, Savannah's, at 749 Marian Anderson. Prior to going into business for herself, she had developed her skills during the war while working for a madam called "Black Susie." According to her daughters, Maudry DeWalt and Marie Price, when their father, T. C. Godeaux, returned home from the war in 1946, he believed that Savannah was working as a barmaid. "He soon learned of her real profession, however, and left her," said Maudry. "But, after six months, he decided he liked the money and came back home," where he often served as Mr. Mom.[22]

Savannah managed her business away from home and family, and tried to protect her daughters by sending them away to a Catholic boarding school in Lafayette, Louisiana. In fact, only when Maudry returned to Port Arthur before Marie was born and attended Lincoln High School did she learn of her mother's profession. One day after an assembly program in which the principal of the school spoke out against the many brothels in town, some of the students kidded her. "When I went home and told her," Maudry said, "she marched up to school and bawled the principal out. That's when I found out what my mother actually did. I cried a lot and was a loner, so it wasn't long before I went back to boarding school."

Growing up in Port Arthur, Maudry felt the sting from not only her mother's profession, but also her light skin. "It wasn't so bad in Louisiana," she said, "because there were a lot more kids who were like us."[23]

Although Savannah operated her business in an old house, she decorated the front room to resemble a nightclub, complete with a jukebox, red-colored booths along one wall, and red valances over the windows. She employed approximately seven girls and welcomed only whites. "Mother didn't like black men," said Marie. "She said they talked too much and didn't have no damn money."[24]

When customers entered, they could pick a girl, dance to the music and visit in one of the booths as long as they were drinking alcoholic beverages. "She made most of her money from selling drinks from the bar," Maudry said. "It was one dollar for a straight shot. The girls, though, were not allowed to drink while working. They could drink cokes or tea."[25] Although Savannah usually dressed at night in sequined dresses, most of her girls dressed scantily.

Being a shrewd businesswoman, Savannah kept track of her entire operation, especially the finances. When a customer stayed all night, the fee was $100; for ten minutes, it was $10; for an hour, it was $25. "If the customer stayed longer than he was supposed to, Mother would knock on the door, and he'd better have more money ready," said Maudry.[26]

Occasionally, men appeared at Savannah's with their wives, and Savannah would call her husband to be with them. "She told everybody that he was her brother," continued Maudry. "One lady, who had a place of business in town, would go there alone and ask for him all the time."[27]

Savannah's prosperous business enabled all the members of her family to spend money freely. They lived in a nice house, bought expensive furniture from Hampton Furniture Store, had their clothes specially made, and drove only the finest of cars. Local citizens often saw Savannah driving around town in her Cadillac Eldorado, wearing a driving jacket with the collar pulled up and gloves on, not wanting the sun to touch her skin. "She had hazel-colored eyes and rubbed bleaching cream on all the time," said Maudry, "because she didn't want to be any darker than she had to be."[28]

Like all the other illegal business proprietors in Jefferson County, Savannah had to pay the police a monthly fee to stay in operation. "Mother paid $650 a month," Marie said, "and sometimes they'd round everybody up and put them in jail, just to make people think they were doing their job. I remember going to the jailhouse when I was little and kissing Mama through the bars."[29]

In the early '50s, Savannah and T. C. went their separate ways and eventually divorced. "Mother bought him out of the house, bought him a car, and sent him and his girlfriend to California," said Marie. "Later, she married a German sea captain, but, because he was white and she was black, the police wouldn't allow them to live together. He finally built a house in Sabine Pass, where he had a dump truck business and lived until he died. Mother was his first and only wife."[30]

After the vice investigation in 1961, the IRS heavily fined Savannah and many of the other madams in Jefferson County for back taxes. Savannah lost her money. To make ends meet, she worked for several years as a care giver for the elderly before suffering several strokes and becoming bedridden. Her daughters cared for her until her death at age 87.

Both Maudry and Marie agreed that when the money was plentiful, they had a very good life. "I think Mother gave away more money in her lifetime than most people ever made," said Marie. "Not only did she move her mother and sisters to Port Arthur and take care of them, but she was always buying clothes and things for poor people. She was a wonderful mother."[31]

From the gambling clubs to the brothels, the madams and club operators in South Jefferson County provided their sort of entertainment for seamen from tankers in port, shift workers at the plants, and the locals who wanted a little action. Perhaps they operated under the watchful eyes of law enforcement officers; nevertheless, police and constables knew where to find them when it was time to round them up in token raids. By the early 1960s, however, the climate was right for a healthy cleanup. Many people in south county, like their counterpart in Beaumont, had had enough. They saw change coming, and they welcomed it.

The Green House in Port Arthur
—Courtesy the Port Arthur Historical Society

Match cover from the Midship Hotel in Port Arthur.

—Courtesy the Port Arthur
Historical Society

Grace Woodyard and her son, Jimmie, in the early 1940s.
—Courtesy Sharon Woodyard Leamons and Pam Woodyard Escobedo

Grace and Rusty Woodyard, circa 1941.
—Courtesy Sharon Woodyard Leamons and Pam Woodyard Escobedo

Marcella Chadwell
—Courtesy the Port Arthur
Historical Society

Marcella and Guy Chadwell
—Courtesy Tim Knight

An evening at Savannah's in Port Arthur
—Courtesy Maudry DeWalt

Savannah Godeaux as a young woman
—Courtesy Maudry DeWalt

Wedding portrait of Maudry DeWalt, Savannah's daughter
—Courtesy Maudry DeWalt

PART III

Concerned Citizens
Speak Out

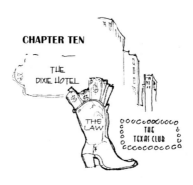

CHAPTER TEN

The Reform Movement Begins in Earnest

Former Beaumont Assistant Chief of Police Clyde Rush recalled being frequently approached in the mid-1950s by leading citizens in Jefferson County who asked him why he didn't try to do something to end the vice and corruption in the area. At the time, he retorted, "You criticize a little old captain with the police department, but you ain't got guts to get up on your feet and try to do something about it."[1]

Around the same time the manager of the *Beaumont Journal* assigned a young reporter by the name of Allan R. Wegemer to cover the nightly news at the police department. He often rode with Officer Rush, whose duty was to patrol the streets of Beaumont at night. Rush remembered a conversation he had one night with the reporter. "He said that he once heard an official of the first newspaper where he worked comment that the political situation of a town could be judged by the cleanliness of its streets. After looking at all the litter everywhere, I answered him by saying, 'Well, this is a filthy S.O.B.' Then I told him, 'You've got a pen. Why don't you do something about it?'"[2] Whether the challenging comment made by Clyde Rush prompted Wegemer into action will never be known, but the young reporter, who had already heard about the county's prevalent vice conditions, soon decided to conduct his own personal investigation. After witnessing what he considered a vulgar display of open vice at many of the existing gambling establishments, Wegemer wrote a series of stories describing his first-hand observations. The stories appeared on the front page of the *Journal* from November 1 to December 13, 1955.[3]

Despite the visible location of Wegemer's articles and their controversial nature, the reporter's work prompted little action. Aside from a statement from The Women's Christian Temperance Union, which expressed disappointment in the apathetic response of the district attorney's office, no citizens seemed inspired by his revelations. Wegemer then decided to file complaints with the district attorney's office himself. The grand jury no-billed Wegemer's complaints, stating that his allegations were "entirely and absolutely without foundation," and that "the newspaper stories which appeared were fashioned from pure imagination—a reporter's pipe dream!"[4]

Having failed to stir up any action with his gambling complaints, but determined to make an impression upon the people of Beaumont and Port Arthur, Wegemer next made an inquiry into prostitution in Jefferson County. He visited 16 houses in the two cities, where he witnessed the widespread sale of beer and liquor to underage boys and saw prostitutes who appeared to be no older than teenagers. This time Wegemer took his complaints to a justice of the peace. The elected officer nonchalantly informed him that no justice of peace had ever taken such action against juvenile drinking and prostitution before or even attempted to do so.

As a final effort, Wegemer sought the help of the Beaumont City Council, which offered him nothing but polite rejection. Shortly after his appearance before the council, his superiors at the *Journal* advised Wegemer to seek employment elsewhere.[5]

Although the evidence that Wegemer presented apparently fell onto the blind eyes of almost everyone in Jefferson County, three members of the April 1955 term grand jury had already taken steps toward reform. George W. Parks, Jr., Thomas F. Sparks and Jim Gibbons were fully aware of the situation that had stymied Wegemer. They were incensed over the type of cases the district attorney actually presented to members of their grand jury for deliberation, rather than real offenses that needed to be considered for indictments. "We felt that we were all intelligent men in the community, and it was an insult to hear the cases presented to us," said Parks, who was district manager of Mutual of Omaha.[6] Parks remembered one trivial case brought before his grand jury that involved an elderly man who had given another man a dog. The man who received the dog trained it and then sold the dog for $50. The elderly man wanted to sue the man for the $50 as he claimed that he stole the dog from him in the first place. "We received $5 a day to go up there and listen to such tripe as that," said Parks.[7]

Convinced that Judge Owen Lord and District Attorney Ramie Griffin controlled their grand jury, Parks, Sparks, and Gibbons decided they would try to bring about reform during their tenure. After they unsuccessfully appealed to Judge Lord to make some changes in the grand jury system, they went to Austin to meet with Attorney General Will Wilson. "When we arrived, it seemed that he knew more about us than we knew about ourselves," said Parks. "We knew then that Judge Lord had gotten hold of Wilson and told him what was going on. When we came back, we organized the Grand Jury Association."[8]

After Parks and others formed the Grand Jury Association two or three representatives from the organization always met surreptitiously with each newly impaneled grand jury. They presented each juror with a booklet that explained his role in the legal system. "We wanted them to know what their duties and their responsibilities were instead of just being pawns," said Parks. "It took a long time before we got a grand jury to pay attention to us. When we did, it didn't take long before the James Committee came down here."[9]

The Grand Jury Association members wanted to make sure their hard work would be continued by the July 1960 term grand jury. George Parks recounted to the incoming grand jurors his "yellow dog case" and explained the heavy burden they carried in maintaining the integrity of the grand jury system in the community. Inspired by his words, Evans Cappel, a local pipefitter, James C. "Huck" Barry, owner of Barry and Sons Sand Company, and Walter Juncker, a Beaumont CPA, decided that their grand jury would take the reform movement even further.[10]

Cappel was a permanent member of Pipefitters Local 195, and was not afraid of losing his job. He started visiting the different clubs and "houses" in the area and reporting back to the jury members. Armed with this information, the three men proposed their strategy. First, Barry would contact various high officials who they believed might be receptive to reform. Next, Juncker and Cappel would arrange meetings with area civic and church groups at which "I would introduce Cappel, and he would give them a first-hand account of what he saw," said Juncker. "He [Cappel] also began writing letters to the newspapers, and I contacted Bob Akers, editor-in-chief of the *Enterprise* and *Journal* and W. W. Ward, managing editor of the *Journal*, both of whom I knew well."

Although Juncker was encouraged during the fall of 1960 that people throughout the community had begun to join in the reform movement, he was surprised when some ministers, apparently fearful of offending certain members within their congregations, hesitated to get involved. "I [then] went to John Wesley Hardt at First Methodist [in Beaumont], who was the newly elected head of the Ministerial Alliance," said Juncker. "He immediately stepped forward, even though he also had various law officials on his roll."[11]

The aggressive efforts made by the few individuals of Jefferson County, who were unafraid to take a stand against the prevalent vice operations existing in their community, were applauded by many other citizens and encouraged the Texas Legislative Investigating Committee to unanimously authorize an undercover investigation in October 1960.[12] Industrial officials, alarmed over increasing acts of violence at the picket lines by union workers and frustrated by the lack of help from local law enforcement, quickly gave the reformers their nods of approval. School officials, who had experienced more problems with juvenile delinquency, and Jefferson County businessmen, who realized that the state of local corruption kept many large northern companies from choosing their port towns for business, were equally pleased to learn that a reform movement had started.[13]

In a letter written to the *Beaumont Enterprise* entitled, "In 1960 Jefferson County was a Stinkhole," Evans Cappel reminisced about his undercover work.

> After several days of routine cases, this [July 1960 term] grand jury wanted to investigate vice conditions. Dist. Atty. Ramie Griffin said that there were no vice conditions, that Jefferson County was clean.
>
> Three of us decided to find out for ourselves. I was one. The

other two were James C. Barry and Walter Juncker . . . We each chipped in some money and made a pot for expenses. With this money, I visited the cathouses and nightclubs throughout Jefferson County. I am a man with a pretty strong constitution. But what I found made me sick . . . There were nightclubs in Beaumont and Port Arthur, and throughout Jefferson County which stayed open all night.

Do you know who their customers were after midnight? Kids.

In August 1960, one night in a nightclub in Beaumont I saw two teenage boys and a teenage girl, all three drunk. What those boys were doing to that drunken girl in plain sight of about 30 or 40 other kids more or less drunk, and a few adults, was a sin and disgrace.

I could not do anything about it at this time, for to do anything would destroy my usefulness as an investigator, so I called up Barry and Juncker to come out and see this. At 4 A.M. in the morning they arrived at the nightclub. They can verify every word and add to it.

But in 1960 in one after another of the bar rooms on main highways and on side roads in the county, both inside and out-side incorporated areas, there were girls to be had for a price . . . These girls operated as waitresses. But what they really sold was delivered in rooms upstairs, or in the back, or many times in trailer houses parked in back of the bar rooms. They didn't care what age their customers were as long as they had the money. . . .

I suffered criticism and abuse for doing what I did when it be-came known. Once in Port Arthur I was attacked and beaten so severely that I had to go to the hospital. Then they tried to pin it on me that I started the fight. It took a jury just seven minutes to find that wasn't so.[14]

Although Wegemer's efforts to bring about immediate change were unsuccessful, the actions of the newly formed grand jury as-sociation kept alive the notion that informed citizens could do something about vice and corruption in the community. Its work and that of other groups encouraged a climate change in Jefferson County. Finally, people began to question the status quo.

*Beaumont CPA Walter C. Juncker
in the 1950s*
    —Courtesy Walter C. Juncker

*Members and officials of the April 1955 Jefferson County Criminal District Court
Grand Jury. Left to right, seated: L. Chambers; L. C. Kyburg; Judge Owen M. Lord;
W. A. Weathers, foreman; Barbara Scoff, secretary; George W. Parks, Jr.; F. B.
Ackerman; R. M. "Reggie" Newton. Standing: E. B. "Ed" Vincent; Frank Adams,
assistant district attorney; Percy Riffle; Tom F. Sparks; Ramie Griffin, district attor-
ney; Jim Gibbons; C. Mullin; James McGrath, assistant district attorney; and G. Ellis
"Bubba" Gaston, Jr.*

    —Courtesy George W. Parks, Jr.

PART IV

The Public Hearings
January 4-6, 1961

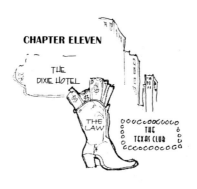

CHAPTER ELEVEN

The Hearings

The First Day

Tom James and the General Legislative Committee tried to ignore the chuckling around town at their expense as they prepared to open three days of publicly televised hearings concerning the results of their investigation. They fully realized the hearings would reveal nothing new to the folks of Jefferson County about the existence and prevalence of vice. Their greater goal was to demonstrate to a skeptical public why law enforcement had allowed vice operations to continue for so long: many of their elected officials had profited handsomely!

Nobody really knew what to expect the morning of January 4, 1961, when testimony began before the House Committee in the Beaumont Federal Building. Televisions were on in almost every home and work place as curious citizens tuned in to watch elected officials explain items on their tax returns and their relationships with known gamblers and madams. Even the administrators at South Park High School in Beaumont assembled their students into the school auditorium to watch the mountain of evidence and testimony taking shape.[1] Perhaps local citizens had not watched television in such great numbers since Elvis Presley made his national television debut on the Ed Sullivan show a few years earlier.

David Witts delivered an opening statement promptly at 9:30 and explained what the hearings hoped to accomplish. The first two days would cover crime and vice conditions as they currently existed in Jefferson County and the effect they had on the citizens. The third day promised to uncover details relating to the system of protection and payoffs in connection with organized crime that allowed such conditions to exist.[2]

C. J. Auten, an intelligence agent with the Department of Public Safety and Sergeant Pete Rogers of the Texas Rangers had both participated in the December 3, 1960, raids. The two officers were among the first to testify. Based on their observations they testified that bookmaking, illegal use of ticker tape machines and tote boards, and the sale of mixed drinks thrived in Jefferson County— facts, of course, that everyone watching already knew. The third witness of the day M. S. Rollo, the local manager of Western Union, confirmed that no reports or complaints regarding improper use of such equipment had ever been filed with his department.[3]

But the testimony from Allan R. Wegemer, the former *Beaumont Journal* reporter, offered far more entertainment value and began to foreshadow the depth to which public officials were involved. Wegemer had lost his job after he published several investigative articles that chronicled his observations of gambling and prostitution in Beaumont in November 1955. Now a police reporter in San Antonio, he testified to the committee that his own attempt to obtain prosecution of charges, which he filed in 1955 in connection with gambling and prostitution, was unsuccessful. He recounted an incident after one late night visit to a "plush casino" in the Spindletop Motel, when James McGrath, a friend of his who also was an assistant district attorney under Ramie Griffin, approached him. When Wegemer explained to McGrath what he was doing at the casino, McGrath warned the intrepid reporter to stop his covert foray into area vice. "It wouldn't be wise for you," McGrath said. "You don't know what you're dealing with." Despite McGrath's well-meaning advice, Wegemer testified, he continued his investigation, observing 30-50 people at a time making bets in gambling joints. He also witnessed the sale of mixed drinks to teenagers in houses of prostitution.

Wegemer then described his encounter with the Jefferson County grand jury. The foreman, whom the reporter described as "hostile," actually prevented Wegemer from showing the evidence he had compiled over the months. An exasperated Wegemer summed up his experience with the committee: "I had beat my head against a legal stone wall, and I figured this whole thing was going to end without a shot in the arm."[4]

Another witness found himself in a similar situation. J. D. Read of the Beaumont Police Department reported to his superiors that he saw gambling in Fuller's Oyster Bar in mid-1954. After the incident, Read recalled, he was handed a number of career setbacks, first, having his patrol area moved to a deserted area far from downtown. It was at this remote location that a concerned citizen approached Read about gambling at Rich's place. After he personally observed gambling in the club, Read reported his discovery to his superiors once again. Shortly thereafter, he testified, his superiors demoted him to the position of dog catcher.[5]

Chief Petty Officer Ray Lighthall of Orange and Mrs. A. W. Lightfoot of Beaumont had also complained about vice conditions in Jefferson County. They described how they were frustrated from the lack of response they received at every level from court officials to the state attorney general's office. When he realized that his complaints landed on deaf ears in Jefferson County, Lighthall made an appointment in Austin with Riley Eugene Fletcher, an assistant to Attorney General Wilson. There he presented his evidence on vice conditions in Orange and Jefferson counties. Mr. Fletcher assured Mr. Lighthall he would handle the evidence properly and get back to him. Mr. Lighthall never heard anything about it again.[6]

Mrs. Lightfoot recounted a similar experience with Riley Fletcher. Like Lighthall, Mrs. Lightfoot had visited with Fletcher and corresponded with him several times by mail. After being frustrated by a few thank you notes from Fletcher, she demanded a statement from him about his office's progress regarding her complaints. Finally, Mr. Fletcher wrote a letter and informed her that his men were doing work in the field. He then advised her to destroy the letter.[7]

After that, a variety of alleged owners, employees, and patrons from the various clubs that committee investigators had raided during the previous month were paraded before the committee.[8] Upon the advice of their attorneys all of the witnesses invoked the Fifth

Amendment and supplied only nonessential information.[9] This placed the committee in a precarious situation. If it compelled the witnesses to testify, they would probably be granted immunity from prosecution, and the committee chose not to take the risk.[10] L. L. "Jack" Thompson, reputedly known as the kingpin of local gamblers, took the Fifth Amendment 17 times during questioning by the committee. Thompson refused to confirm whether he operated the Pen Yan Club and refused to identify pictures of the club and its employees. He likewise declined to identify his brother, whom the officers arrested along with Thompson during the December 3 raid on the Pen Yan Club.[11]

During the investigation, committee members had obtained records of phone calls made from the various establishments, which came under scrutiny after the December raids. At the hearings, Witts produced an analysis of those records which indicated extensive telephone traffic between bookies in Jefferson County and known bookmaking establishments all over the country, for gambling on sporting events. This provided more evidence, Witts insisted, that organized bookmaking and gambling in Jefferson County reached nationwide.[12]

One of the most compelling witnesses to testify during the first day of the public hearings was Russell Bond, a primary player in the numbers racket. Bond explained to the committee that during his years running the lottery-like game he encountered no interference from the Beaumont Police Department because of the payoff. Around the first of every month, he said, Jerome A. "Jake" Giles told all partners to kick in some cash, which averaged about $3,000 per month for the years 1950-1957, totaling approximately $252,000. The committee was unable to subpoena Giles, who had been assassinated in broad daylight on Crockett Street by Lee Wesley "Banjo Red" Marshall in 1958. However, state auditors were able to obtain and study the bank records of Small Cars, Inc., a company owned by Giles, and his partners, H. R. Calendar and D. L. Evans, Jr. The records showed large deposits of cash from July to December 24, 1960, totaling approximately $27,000.

Auditors figured that in order to obtain all the cash that these men deposited in the account of Small Cars, Inc., a go-cart race track, it would have been necessary to have an average of 75,000 rides during that period of time. Eliminating 77 days of inclement weather, 700 rides per day would be required to produce the amount of cash that went into the account of Small Cars, Inc. [13] A profitable venture, indeed!

Many of the alleged owners of known brothels in the county had left the area in haste before the officers served their subpoenas. But Savannah Godeaux, the proprietor of Savannah's, did appear before the committee. Her "testimony" revealed little as she demurely insisted before the frustrated committee members, who knew better, that she could not understand their questions because she only spoke French.[14]

The last witness to testify on the first day was Thomas Arthur Wigley, who told the committee of cock fights conducted regularly for years at pits near Pine Tree Lodge on Taylor's Bayou. According to the owner of the lodge, Wigley testified, Sheriff Charley Meyer provided a source of protection for the cock fights, no doubt for a price. The pits had a seating capacity for 200 to 300 people and drew a large revenue for the owner. Wigley told the committee that he once heard the owner mention, "If it wasn't for Charley, I couldn't operate, because that's the only protection I have."[15]

As the first day of the public hearings drew to a close, most dismissed the whole affair as political grandstanding by James, whose dog and pony show revealed nothing that hadn't been common knowledge for years. But the testimony clearly implied more than apathy on the part of local law enforcement officials. Beneath the lighthearted gossip loomed an undercurrent of growing concern as the names of prominent local officials appeared again and again in connection with serious criminal activity that could possibly be tied to national syndicates. It was becoming quite apparent to almost everyone that no matter how humorously its citizens regarded the spectacle going on at the Federal Building, Jefferson County would never be the same when it was over.

The Second Day

The second day of testimony concentrated on some of the less obvious effects of lax law enforcement in Jefferson County. Narcotics trafficking was a criminal activity that was nearly unheard of in the dawn of the new decade. James hoped the sparse evidence of narcotics abuse collected by the committee would provide a wake-up call to the people of Jefferson County about a situation that could affect their children.

In what was clearly a scare tactic, the committee called an unidentified teenage girl as the first witness of the second day. She claimed that she purchased alcohol and drugs that included barbiturates at Beaumont clubs and that she went to the hospital, near death from abusing the substances. The girl implicated a "Dr. Darwin" in connection with the pill supply chain.[16] In his defense, Dr. P.S. Darwin took the stand and admitted to prescribing drugs to an estimated 9,000 patients. Stating that he prescribed drugs mainly to truck drivers who needed to stay awake, he also confessed that he never asked for identification.[17] Ethel Darwin, the doctor's former nurse and ex-wife, implicated Darwin further by recalling in private session that most of Dr. Darwin's patients were under the age of 21 at the time she worked as his nurse. She also remembered orders for "tremendous quantities" of drugs from a supply company in Pennsylvania, up to 10,000 pills at a time.[18] Dr. Darwin withheld all records from the Pennsylvania company on the grounds that they might incriminate him, but he admitted that he did not keep a careful check on his patients or require that his patients see him before he renewed their prescriptions.[19]

W. E. "Dub" Naylor, an agent in charge of the narcotics section of the DPS, insisted during his testimony that Jefferson County remained one of the "top three areas in Texas with a narcotics problem." Naylor and other undercover agents came into Jefferson County on a DPS narcotics investigation, but they quickly left the area when they discovered someone had mysteriously revealed their identities. Naylor believed that narcotics use consisted mostly of marijuana and barbiturates, and that prostitutes accounted for 82 percent of the users.[20]

The consistent failure to prosecute liquor law violations highlighted in the hearings pointed suspiciously to El Roy Mauldin, Jr., the district supervisor for the Texas Liquor Control Board, which included Jefferson and 10 other counties. When it was his turn to testify, Mauldin opened by reading a long prepared statement in which he complained about the limited staff available to him to cover an area in which "approximately 500,000 people lived." James asked Mauldin to recall the last time he requested additional undercover help, but Mauldin responded that he could not remember.[21] John

Crank, special supervisor of the Texas Liquor Control Board, said in later testimony that he had not received a request to place an undercover man in the Beaumont–Port Arthur area in over two years.[22] Mauldin even admitted that liquor dispensing equipment and emptied liquor containers often were returned to owners after his agents had confiscated them; but he quickly added that such returns only occurred in exchange for a small fine and a plea of guilty.[23]

Carl Mass, Jr., an agent working under Mauldin, explained to the public how Mauldin resisted any attempts by his agents to prosecute liquor law violators. Mass was admonished to stay away from the private clubs. "They were here before we came, " Mauldin told his agent, "and they will be here after we've gone." Committee members then asked Mass how he managed to keep busy at a job where Mauldin kept his hands tied. Mass replied, "I was kept fully occupied by reading newspapers and writing letters home."

Mass remembered only one raid conducted during the time he worked in the Beaumont office. Mauldin assigned Mass to hit the Cipango Club on 11th Street in December 1958. As he entered the establishment with other officers, Mass testified, O. B. (Slim) Griffin walked in and demanded, "Does El Roy Mauldin know about this raid?" The raiders confiscated only two cases of partially filled whiskey bottles in the club, but Mauldin had instructed them not to destroy anything. Mass said that he had never seen any confiscated bottles destroyed, as required by Liquor Control Board regulations, while he was working for Mauldin.[24]

Paul Jordan, an inspector stationed in Houston at the time of the hearings, testified that he worked for Mauldin in the southeast Texas district from October 1957 until September 1959. The hierarchy in the Beaumont Police Department rebuked him for raiding the Raven Club after he discovered that the club had violated a city ordinance regarding liquor laws. The officers, Jordan said, told him that the owner of the club provided a "good source of information" in connection with undercover police work. They subsequently instructed Jordan and fellow inspector Dave Cowsert, who also appeared to testify, "not to try to enforce any more city laws." Jordan and Cowsert repeatedly reported to Mauldin complaints they had received regarding the teenage drinking problem at the gambling joints and houses of prostitution, but Mauldin virtually ignored them, insisting again that the inspectors should leave the private clubs alone. On one occasion, Mauldin ordered Cowsert to return a confiscated liquor dispenser to the owner of Bluchie's Paradise, a club in Port Arthur. When Cowsert questioned Mauldin's judgment on the matter, Mauldin answered that State Senator Jep S. Fuller had requested that he return the dispenser.[25] Fuller, the former Jefferson County district attorney, represented not only the operator of Bluchie's Paradise, but also the operators of several others clubs where Texas liquor laws were consistently violated.

The Final Day

Even if the information and shady practices "uncovered" by James and his committee during the investigation failed to astound the public, the stage was set by the testimony from witnesses on the first two days of public hearings. The time had arrived for a showdown of sorts between the old guard of Jefferson County politics and the group of out-of-town crusaders who sought to bring down the curtain on a way of life that had persisted for longer than anyone could recall. The public hearings would leave no doubt that most of the senior locally elected officials were on the take, but just how deep—or how high up the ladder—did the benefits reach? Did the payoff arrangements run all the way to Jep Fuller in the Texas Senate, or even higher? The committee members knew that the hearings would not answer these questions. But they hoped what the people of Jefferson County heard would be so unsettling that they would move to take command of what the committee believed was a situation spiraling out of control.

Sheriff Charley Meyer had enjoyed extreme popularity as a public official for many years, and the committee realized it faced an uphill battle as it attempted to show the people of Jefferson County that their beloved sheriff was a lawbreaker. Meyer's absolute lack of respect for the committee's mission had surfaced earlier when the committee asked him to appear in executive session. There, he admitted knowing Rita Ainsworth and Jack Thompson, the known gambler who took the Fifth Amendment 17 times during the first day of the hearings; he even referred to Thompson as a friend with whom he'd hunted and fished since 1947. When the committee members pressed him about why he refused to uphold the laws regarding gambling in the state of Texas, he responded with his own recalcitrant philosophy: "You can't stop bookmaking," he opined. "I believe an American citizen should be allowed to enjoy his life and act pretty much as he pleases, unless that interferes with somebody else's life."[26]

As the first witness called during the final day of the publicly televised hearings on January 6, Meyer still refused to grant any credibility to the committee. From the start, he attempted to exert his influence over the proceedings by reading a prepared statement with the obvious implication that the committee was wasting everyone's time by focusing its attention on Jefferson County. He acknowledged, in his statement, that drinking, gambling, and prostitution were present in his community just like they were in any community of a similar size, but vehemently denied the existence of "large scale dope operations."[27]

He also explained away any additional income appearing on his tax returns as funds necessary to run for public office, stay in public office, and participate in "worthwhile projects of the community." Then he went on the offensive, calling on all the charm and persuasion that had served him so well in Jefferson County. Meyer knew what his audience cared about, and he pointed out the low incidence of rape, armed robbery, and burglary in Jefferson County as compared to the numbers in Dallas and other communities. This was the reason, he explained, that local officials in Jefferson County didn't waste taxpayer dollars and time on aggressively prosecuting what he called, the "petty offenses" of vice. To lend further credence to his position, he called the process "selective enforcement" and explained that he preferred to use his limited manpower "where it will stop the most crime."[28]

After the committee expressed its appreciation for Sheriff Meyer's "wholesome and reassuring report about crime in Jefferson County," Counsel David Witts proceeded, unaffected, with a relentless interrogation to determine the extent of Meyer's understanding and involvement in the gambling and prostitution problems plaguing the area. Although Meyer made limited admissions about knowing gamblers and occasionally visiting private clubs, Witts' intense questioning failed to reveal more than ineptitude or apathy on the part of the sheriff.

However, when committee members revealed Meyer's income tax returns, they began to paint Meyer into a corner. During the years of 1956-1959, the sheriff's records showed substantial campaign contributions that far exceeded expenses, especially during years he ran unopposed. In years when there weren't any elections, contributions exceeded campaign expenses by more than $30,000. Meyer explained the need for approximately $85,000 in excess of his salary and campaign expenses as "assistance from corporations, labor, and individual businessmen who wished him to remain in office and still have enough money to rear his family."

Meyer also admitted that the contributions often arrived rather unofficially, in envelopes from anonymous sources and not at any specific time. But he refused to further discuss the methods by which he received such contributions or mention the names of any of his supporters, assuring the committee that he had never in any way jeopardized his oath of office. "I'm so grateful when I get a little help to continue my campaign and remain in office, I'm just grateful for the assistance, to tell you the truth about it."

Witts then moved on to the subject of Meyer's involvement in the Texas Sheriffs' Association. As president of the association, the committee presumed that the Jefferson County sheriff had considerable authority over the publication of the *Texas Lawman*. Witts found the advertisement for the Yukon Club especially curious, since the Texas Rangers had seized approximately $14,000 from that same club during a raid only a few weeks earlier. He pointed out advertisements for other clubs, which fell victim to the December raids. Meyer adamantly defended the legitimacy of the publication. He insisted, however, that he had no knowledge of the businesses that advertised in it.[29]

The committee had failed to wrest any earth-shattering admissions from the charismatic sheriff, but it harbored no doubts that eyebrows were raising everywhere when the numbers from his tax returns became public. These numbers revealed more than campaign contributions, especially for a sheriff who, more often than not, ran unopposed.

The testimony of Reagan Baker, constable of Precinct 1 that included Beaumont, and O'Neil Provost, constable of Precinct 2, which included Port Arthur, added further fuel to the fire of suspicion. They also admitted to receiving substantial anonymous campaign contributions, but both figured such gifts were legitimate and reported them on the income tax returns. Under pressure, Provost conceded that his power to shut down vices in the area might have invited contributions by individuals who linked the two together. Baker added that some of the clubs he had visited in the area "did him the courtesy" of shutting down any gambling when he came inside.[30] The chief of police of Port Arthur, Garland Douglas, whose position was appointed, not elected, likewise had a difficult time explaining the $65,000 he received in campaign contributions between 1955 and 1959. Then he stated to the committee that over the past several years he had seen only minimal gambling and only a few liquor law violations, and, further, that prostitution had stopped in the city of Port Arthur. However, the testimony of the next witness, the refreshingly honest Assistant Chief of Police David Phoenius Moore, instantly shattered his credibility.

Moore stated that he personally knew of at least ten houses of prostitution that had been operating in Port Arthur for the past 18 years. He even admitted that he had become acquainted with girls in many of the houses so he could keep the "undesirables" out of the city and thereby hold narcotics traffic to a minimum. The girls made good informants, he said, and this justified his allowing them to remain in business. Moore testified to having seen bars in brothels such as Grace Woodyard's and Marcella's, but had never reported it to the Liquor Control Board or to Douglas because he knew of no laws restricting the sale of liquor in a house of prostitution. He felt that prostitution, gambling, and liquor violations posed no problems to a city like Port Arthur. Such a personal philosophy accounted for Moore's refusal to enforce state laws regarding the offense of prostitution. He said that he never filed a complaint because, in his opinion, he had never seen a violation. Believing he had no direct authority from Douglas to send detectives into the field to investigate vice, the officer never gave him such assignments. His officers did, however, occasionally pick up girls for vagrancy. Moore attributed the few thousand dollars in excess of his salary, which appeared on his returns, to gambling winnings at various conferences, and he claimed he suffered "no losses" in the last several years.[31]

Beaumont Police Chief J. H. "Jim" Mulligan and Chief of Detectives James Stafford blamed politics for the current situation in Jefferson County. Mulligan acknowledged that bookmaking went on at Rich's, the Yukon, the Liberal, the Commodore, and the

Bowie clubs, but he said he hadn't closed them down because "some former Beaumont mayors" asked him not to. He also failed to report known liquor law violations in the clubs or make any arrests because he lacked the necessary funds in his budget to undertake such law enforcement. Mulligan admitted a desire to shut down prostitution in Beaumont, although his "bosses" (whom he declined to identify), thought otherwise.[32]

Stafford also complained about having his hands tied by city officials, who likewise remained nameless. He testified about an incident in which he caught Johnny Angelo, a known gambler. The district attorney released Angelo despite Stafford's objections, telling him he caught "the wrong man, a good ol' boy." Stafford made no other gambling arrests. Stafford also acknowledged being at the Dixie Hotel to check on Miss Rita's girls about 20 times but said he had never made an arrest for prostitution. Stafford insisted that the people of Jefferson County wanted it that way. He would have closed down gambling and prostitution a long time ago, he testified, if the city administration and certain citizens, including the vice president of the First National Bank, had allowed him to.

In spite of his sanctimonious complaining, Stafford appeared to have enjoyed the same benefits as those he sought to implicate. Casey Revia, a former employee at one of the Beaumont clubs, told the committee and viewers that he'd witnessed a series of payoffs between the owner of the club and Stafford that took place every Monday morning.[33]

The carefully crafted machine that enabled gambling, liquor law violations, and prostitution to prosper in Jefferson County was beginning to take shape in the eyes of the viewing public. Meyer's selective enforcement theory was being whittled down and replaced by the realization that vice didn't persist because law enforcement turned a blind eye, but because law enforcement and city officials had actually created a system in which they could prosper—for the right price. Within the county, the system could not be maintained unless it reached to every level of jurisprudence. Thus, Meyer tended to business in the field, while Ramie Griffin and Owen Lord made sure things ran smoothly inside the courthouse doors.

Ramie Griffin had held the office of district attorney in Jefferson County since 1951. During his testimony on the final day of the public hearings, Griffin admitted knowing that a small amount of gambling and prostitution existed in the county, but he said he could not remember any felony gambling convictions or prostitution arrests in 10 years. Griffin could only account for the enduring presence of gambling by stating that he had never personally seen it going on. Although he conceded having visited the Bowie Club in the past and the Pen Yan once to have a mixed drink, Griffin insisted that he had never seen gambling in progress.

Regarding prostitution, Griffin recalled hearing of "Rita's," but he could remember no other names of alleged Beaumont and Port Arthur brothels without the aid of Witts, who listed them for him. Griffin likewise confessed that he had never convicted a person for prostitution during his term, which he explained by saying that no one had ever filed a prostitution complaint with his office. After Representative James reminded him of one specific case, that of Allan Wegemer, Griffin answered simply that he could not recall the reporter's allegations. He maintained that the city police officers, and not district attorneys, carried the responsibility for the administration of the prostitution laws.

James then asked the district attorney about a bank account entitled "Ramie Griffin, Trustee." Griffin explained that the account was part of a check-collecting service he performed under his private law practice. However, the committee pointed out that he performed the service on county time, using county personnel, county equipment, county stationery, and county stamps. Among many other inconsistencies, committee auditors questioned the rather large amounts entered on Griffin's income tax returns, which the district attorney claimed were "gin rummy winnings" and a business venture.[34]

Unlike the lackadaisical district attorney, District Judge Owen M. Lord stated that he felt "shocked and surprised to learn of the situation" in Jefferson County. To his knowledge, he told James, there had been no gambling complaints filed during the past 30 years.[35] Judge Lord long before had set up a grand jury system in which it was rare for the district attorney to file complaints or for a grand jury to hear of them. At the time of the hearings, Texas law required a district judge to select five grand jury commissioners from different parts of the county. The commissioners convened their meeting in a room where each member selected four people to compile a list of 20 individuals. The commissioners selected the first 12 people from the list to serve as grand jury members, providing none of them had a legitimate excuse not to serve. The judge then selected a foreman and an assistant foreman. Under the system in Jefferson County, Judge Lord, District Attorney Ramie Griffin and Sheriff Meyer selected three commissioners from a list of their friends who were called upon to perform the service again and again. The commissioners selected by Griffin and Meyer chose the final list of 20 names from which Lord took the final 12 names. So-called "friends of the court," these people served a term of three months, during which they heard cases presented to them by the district attorney.

One former "friend of the court" recalled that the district attorney always advised the jurors as to his feelings about each case. When confronted by the committee about this highly unorthodox method of conducting grand jury proceedings, Griffin told the committee that he offered his opinion to the grand jurors about whether he thought a case would be worth the effort or just a waste of taxpayer's money. "If the sheriff, the district attorney or the district judge wanted someone no-billed," recalled the former grand juror, "the district attorney simply expressed his desire." Such a low incidence of indictments gave the appearance that no problems existed.[36]

Lord asserted before the committee that although he would have rather chosen grand jurors in the traditional method, the same grand jurors had been re-appointed over and over because of the difficulty of finding good men to serve in that capacity. In an attempt to deflect blame from himself and in the direction of the district attorney, Lord testified that he had informed the grand juries they could exclude the district attorney from the proceedings if they wanted to, but that Griffin had told jurors otherwise. Lord also told committee members that he had instructed each grand jury to look into all the problems of vice and gambling, and yet none had returned any indictments to him. Lord also claimed not to understand that, as a judge, he had the power to use injunctive power to stop vice.[37]

The final witnesses to appear before the committee expressed deep concern about the deteriorating situation in Jefferson County. Joe Wilkinson, a member of a recent grand jury that met during the first term of 1960, gave a first-hand account of a personal incident that illustrated the threatening nature of the corrupt political machine that had dominated Beaumont and Port Arthur for so long. A few days after Wilkinson had expressed the desire to fight crime actively in Jefferson County during one of the highly secret grand jury deliberations, a man approached him in his office at the Port Arthur Bank, where Wilkinson was vice president. The visitor asked Wilkinson not to pursue the matter further, stating that such an operation would hurt many of his friends politically. The man then added persuasively that if Wilkinson loved his wife and family, he had "better get off that line of thought." The bank vice president had no idea which grand jury member had leaked the information so rapidly.[38]

George W. Parks, Jr., Jim Gibbons, and Tom F. Sparks, founding members of the Grand Jury Association, corroborated Joe Wilkinson's story of corruption within the county and told of their frustrations when they served as grand jury members. From the onset, they testified, the actions of District Judge Owen Lord and District Attorney Ramie Griffin thwarted the association members' efforts by preventing gambling or prostitution cases from being presented to the grand jury, especially in 1955, the year Allan Wegemer waged his crusade.

The Grand Jury Association founders also ascertained that if a member of any grand jury expressed an interest in community welfare, particularly in connection with the gambling and vice conditions in Jefferson County, that the commissioners would not call him to serve as a grand juror again. Placing the blame for this squarely on the shoulders of Judge Owen Lord, they explained how he indirectly controlled the entire grand jury process by repeatedly selecting the same three men as commissioners, who, in turn, selected only "tame" individuals to serve as grand jurors. The association members testified that in spite of their appeal to Lord to select grand juries in compliance with Texas law, the judge consistently refused. The three founders of the Grand Jury Associaton on occasion suggested to District Attorney Ramie Griffin that another district judge other than Judge Lord might shoulder the responsibility for selecting grand jury members. The district attorney likewise ignored this recommendation, they said.[39]

As the final day of testimony on Friday, January 6, was winding down, three committee members presented closing statements. Vice Chairman James, the first to speak, began by saying that he regarded the entire process as a great success. He attributed the accomplishment in large measure to the citizens of the community who came together and aided the committee with its efforts, in particular the churches and the Ministerial Association, along with various civic groups and other private individuals who came forth with information. He expressed ardent admiration for the courage of the people who testified despite threats to themselves and their families.[40]

Counselor Witts followed James, adding his thanks to the citizens of Jefferson County. He made a point of saying that the situation in the area existed as the result of police protection. He said he understood that no citizen of Jefferson County, despite reports to the contrary, "is so apathetic, no community so unconcerned, as to welcome the spectacle of open gambling, open saloons and open bawdy houses." In his final comments, he again urged the citizens watching to look beyond the apparent corruption of their local officials and consider whether something larger played a part in maintaining the conditions that allowed vice to prosper.

"There are two hallmarks of organized crime," he insisted, "violence to maintain internal discipline and keep out competition, and second, the securing of immunity from law enforcement. Wherever these are found, they constitute unmistakable evidence of the existence of an organized terminal underworld, which serves as a function of local government and establishes a ruthless and violent control over the community where it exists."[41]

The House Committee Investigating Committee now had fulfilled one of its primary objectives, to educate area citizens about unlawful conditions that existed in their local governments in the county. Over the subsequent years they would learn that the vice and corruption that plagued their community could be brought under control by dedicated public officials and the patient application of laws. The hearings finally had awakened the citizens of Jefferson County to the task at hand.

Counselor David Witts, standing, questions Beaumont Police Chief Jim Mulligan on the first day of the public hearings.

—Courtesy the Tyrrell Historical Library.

Former Beaumont Journal *reporter Allan Wegemer as he testified on the first day of the Texas House of Representatives Investigating Committee public hearings.*
—Microfilm photo from the *Beaumont Enterprise.*
Courtesy the Beaumont Public Library

Below: *Sheriff Charley Meyer as he testified on the third day of the public hearings.*
—Microfilm photo from
the *Beaumont Enterprise.*
Courtesy the Beaumont Public Library

Above: *Tom James and Port Arthur Police Chief Garland B. Douglas on the third day of the public hearings.*
—Microfilm photo from
the *Beaumont Enterprise.*
Courtesy the Beaumont Public Library

The Jefferson County Parade

Rumors were thick, times were trying,
You could hear everything but the truth and meat a frying.

Mr. James and Mr. Witts were coming to town,
They were going to turn things upside down.

They set up shop in the old P.O.,
But all you could hear was "I don't know."

They all got set and the parade did begin,
They had a question for all the men.

They took the 5th about 99 times,
Why tell the story about all the crimes.

They had a pill doc thrown in their lap,
You could get a goof ball if you had a truck and a cap.

Up came the big shots from the sheriff on down,
You could just find that money thrown around..

It came in envelopes both white and brown,
You could find it in the car while parked uptown.

Then came the police chief who said it twice,
He had a sister who was awful nice.

Up came his assistant who couldn't be fired,
He would enforce the law if it made him tired.

Following up was a nice young man,
Who saw the pay off put in his hand.

Then came Ramie with a story to tell,
But his books they just couldn't jell.

Ramie he said it wasn't a sin,
For the ole D.A. to play a little gin.

Up stood the law from Port Arthur,
But all they could do was stammer and stutter.

If you ran a beer joint in the town, they say,
To the Marine Guard Service you would have to pay

Now Mr. Maulding was a man who licked inflation,
You could live on $40.00 per month anywhere in the nation.

You see, we really don't know what's taking place,
Nobody can find Rita and Grace.

There is a new record out, they are playing the song,
Poor ole Blue Buddy has done and gone.

Now Uncle Sam's boys, they are on the spot,
They have a way of telling just what you got.

—Author unknown. Courtesy R. T. Fertitta, Jr.

PART V

The Cleanup Process

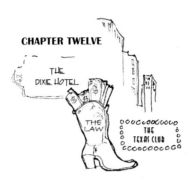

CHAPTER TWELVE

The Demands Mount—
And the Heads Begin to Roll

As the three days of televised General Legislative Investigating Committee hearings came to an end, the people of Jefferson County found themselves in a state of shock. The real source of disbelief among Jefferson County residents concerned the mystery money, the so-called campaign contributions, which lucky officials found on their desks and in their cars, placed there by anonymous donors. Those who had blindly relied on their public officials to uphold the law for decades shook their heads in confusion, wondering whom they could trust.

Bob Akers, editor-in-chief of the *Beaumont Enterprise,* and W. W. Ward, managing editor of the *Beaumont Journal*, wasted no time in addressing the situation. Their editorials challenged readers to contemplate seriously the "revelations" presented by the investigating committee and asked, what would the citizens do as a result of the investigation and hearings? Everyone wondered whether this signaled a turning of the tide or business as usual.[1] Eager to capitalize on the intense public interest generated by the hearings and the call for reform, the editorials proclaimed, "we have, indeed, a rendezvous with our collective conscience."[2]

Immediately, a wave of public sentiment condemning the vice

conditions and apparent breakdown of law enforcement in Jefferson County began to surface throughout the community. The church, silent or stifled for years, led the charge. John W. Hardt, the newly elected president of the Beaumont Ministers' Association, stated that the official board of his church adopted a resolution supporting and encouraging the investigation. His sentiments seemed to parallel those of the most concerned citizens in the area: "I hope and believe that the public will not take [the hearings] as a laughing matter, or as one about which nothing can be done, but will demand responsible law enforcement."[3]

E. W. Vanhoozer, secretary of the Beaumont Ministers' Association and general secretary of the Beaumont YMCA, also expressed the opinion that the result of the investigation would depend upon what the citizens did about the situation. Mrs. Bill Peveto, president of the Beaumont City Council PTA, representing 30 PTAs around the city, stated that the next meeting of her group would result in the adoption of a resolution in praise of the investigation. Finally, William R. Tucker, then associate professor of government at Lamar Tech, charged the public with the responsibility for the future of its town. He proclaimed "the future should prove to be a point of departure for the city of Beaumont. No doubt it will be a sharp break with the past."[4]

The sentiments of the newspaper editors and community leaders were soon echoed by many other churches and civic organizations throughout the area. Most of them adopted formal resolutions requesting that "those with the proper authority" remove from office those who admitted knowledge of law violations. Groups sent copies of the resolutions to James, the Jefferson County sheriff's office, the office of the district attorney, the city council, the speaker of the House of Representatives, and area news media.[5] While leaders of the community worked diligently to address the problems at hand, some of the more light-hearted citizens placed signs in the back windows of their automobiles that read, "Throw your white envelopes in here."[6]

Members of the Wesbury Sunday School Class of Asbury United Methodist Church on East Lucas Street in Beaumont expressed themselves vividly in a four-point program of action, which they sent to the Beaumont City Council, the Beaumont newspapers and Representative James. In it, they requested:

1. A clean slate of capable, trustworthy men in positions of authority in the law enforcement agencies. Past performance of present officials indicate that they are not likely to meet these qualifications.
2. Some continuing assurance in the form of public reports that the law is being upheld.
3. Organization of a vice squad within the city of Beaumont, the activities of which would appear in the above mentioned report.
4. A permanent halt of all gambling, prostitution, liquor, and narcotics violations.[7]

At the same time, editor Bob Akers requested a statement from Attorney General Will Wilson outlining procedures for the dismissal of key elected officials involved in the vice operations. This time the attorney general's office promptly responded, and Attorney General Wilson's answer appeared in print for the benefit of everyone who expressed concern about certain officials remaining in office:

> The citizens cannot achieve the recall of an elected official by circulating petitions, however, an individual citizen may bring suit for removal of the sheriff, district attorney or constable and in some cases, a district judge may remove any of the three officers mentioned above. A citizen's suit for removal of a sheriff or constable must have the consent of the district attorney before the attorney general can participate in removal proceedings.

The removal procedures described in the state laws placed Ramie Griffin in an awkward position. Wilson later added that the laws remained unclear in reference to the removal of the district attorney because there was no precedent or example in Texas courts for the removal of the district attorney. Despite the vagueness of state law on this point, Wilson believed the judge of the district court possessed the authority to remove the D.A.[8]

Meanwhile, angry citizens demanded that the officeholders who had escaped the attention of the investigating committee act quickly and decisively to rid Jefferson County of its corrupt officials. On January 10, 1961, Beaumont City Manager Jack Jeffrey dismissed Beaumont Chief of Police Jim Mulligan from office after

Mulligan unsuccessfully tried to suspend Chief of Detectives Jim Stafford. The Beaumont police chief became the first casualty of the investigation.[9]

Following the dismissal of Mulligan on January 11, the Beaumont City Council appointed Willie Bauer, a 22-year veteran of the Beaumont police force, to Mulligan's position. After first declining to accept the position in the heat of the circumstances that surrounded his superior's dismissal, Bauer soon reconsidered. On January 12, Chief Bauer announced the formation of the Special Services Vice Squad to enforce gambling, prostitution, and narcotics laws and ordinances. He then moved quickly to suspend Jim Stafford for "neglect of duty" and "conduct prejudicial to good order." Bauer alleged specifically that Stafford entered a "bawdy house," later identified as the Marine Hotel at 224 Tevis, on or about November 2, 1960. The charge contended that Stafford, by his actions, "indicated and exemplified" to other officers that he "approved of and condoned law violations involving prostitution."[10] Stafford appealed to the Civil Service Commission, arguing his suspension was "politically motivated." The Civil Service Commission upheld the suspension of the former chief of detectives, but Stafford continued to fight all the way to the Ninth Court of Civil Appeals. His fate was finally settled on March 1, 1962, when the appellate court upheld the decision to fire him.[11]

On January 11, 1961, Port Arthur City Manager Charles Brazil announced the discharges of Port Arthur Chief of Police Garland B. Douglas and Assistant Chief D. P. Moore in response to demands made during a city commission meeting attended by scores of outraged citizens. A few minutes after the commission recessed, Douglas tendered his resignation, stating, "In order to save the city commission any embarrassment, I resign as of now." Detective Chief Glenn Hamman took over the position of chief of police in Port Arthur.[12]

On Sunday, January 15, Representative James and Counselor Witts returned to Jefferson County to speak to a standing-room-only audience of about 2,000 enthusiastic citizens in the auditorium of Woodrow Wilson Junior High School in Port Arthur. During their visit, the two investigators addressed the newly organized Citizens Betterment Committee of Greater Port Arthur. Warning that "your enemies will try to divert your attention from the crusade,"[13] James told the organization that "the great common purpose now is law enforcement and the proper moral climate."[14]

Also on January 15, District 2 of the Women's Christian Temperance Union authorized a request to Coke Stevenson, Jr., the head of the State Liquor Control Board. In it they asked for the dismissal of Beaumont District Supervisor El Roy Mauldin, Jr., because of the evidence revealed during the public hearings. The women's group expressed exceptional concern about reports regarding the accessibility of alcohol to minors.[15] Stevenson responded by authorizing an investigation into the conduct of Mauldin. Shortly thereafter, Stevenson announced that he had decided to transfer El Roy Mauldin, Jr., to San Antonio and that Joseph R. McDaniel, the San Antonio senior inspector, would replace Mauldin in Beaumont.[16]

On February 2, Port Arthur's Civil Service Commission reinstated D. P. Moore. The order carried with it restoration of the officer's full pay and seniority. Legal counsel for the Civil Service Commission, joined by the attorneys representing Moore, contended that Brazil's charge against Moore could not justify suspension. Aside from that point, they argued, the city manager did not have the authority to suspend an assistant chief of police under the city charter. Quentin Keith, who served as counsel for four of the witnesses during the hearings, including recently relocated El Roy Mauldin, Jr., also served as special counsel for the Civil Service Commission. Keith insisted that under the charter, "only the chief of police can suspend a policeman."[17]

Area church groups took one of the strongest stances against crime in the area, expressing their demands at nearly every meeting and publishing them in every newspaper around. Before the public hearings, recalled Bishop John Wesley Hardt, the Beaumont Ministers' Association had been a small, inactive group. Energized by the prospect of its role in the reform, the group was totally transformed from about half a dozen preachers in attendance to about 40 or 50. As a signal of its commitment to change, the Ministers' Association invited two black ministers to participate, the Reverend G. W. Daniels of the Sunlight Baptist Church and the Reverend McCarty of the Starlight Baptist Church.[18]

Local news media began calling this new chapter in Beaumont's crime story "Church versus Vice," as clergymen representing some 35,000 Christians and Jews demanded that the Beaumont City Council "clean house and keep it clean."[19] Because of his role in the reform effort, Bishop Hardt received threatening telephone calls warning, "You better watch your children. There are people who are not pleased with your speaking out." Hardt recalled that about a dozen members left his church in protest. But others remained active, notably Gilbert Adams, the lawyer who represented Charley Meyer. Hardt also remembered Judge Owen Lord, who had been on the church rolls for years but had never attended, suddenly started showing up. "Providence and circumstances put me in a position at that time that I felt compelled to respond to," said Hardt. "I feel that eternal vigilance is the price of freedom."[20]

Willie Bauer was appointed Beaumont chief of police on January 11, 1961, by the Beaumont City Council.
—Courtesy the Beaumont
Police Department

Tom James, left, and David Witts confer before an appearance at a citizens public meeting in Port Arthur on January 15, 1961.

—Microfilm photo from
the *Beaumont Enterprise.*
Courtesy the Beaumont Public Library

Jim STAFFORD, Appellant,

v.

FIREMEN'S AND POLICEMEN'S CIVIL
SERVICE COMMISSION OF the CITY
OF BEAUMONT, Texas, Appellee.

No. 6530.

Court of Civil Appeals of Texas.

Beaumont.

March 1, 1962..

Reported was the judgment of the Ninth Court of Civil Appeals that upheld the discharge of Jim Stafford, Vol. 355, South Western Reporter, 2d Series, page 555.

Proceeding involving discharge of inspector of detectives. The District Court, Jefferson County, Harold R. Clayton, J., entered a judgment confirming the detective's discharge by the Civil Service Commission and the detective appealed. The Court of Civil Appeals, Stephenson, J., held that the police officer's failure to make complaint respecting existence of prostitutes subjected him to removal regardless of any alleged instructions from a superior officer, and there was substantial evidence to support decision that detective was properly dismissed for conduct prejudicial to good order.

Affirmed.

Reverend John Wesley Hardt was elected president of the Beaumont Ministers' Association in January 1961. Under his leadershhip the association grew to become a strong voice in the reform movement.

—Courtesy Bishop John Wesley Hardt

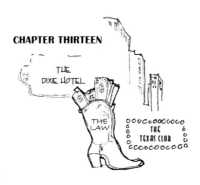

CHAPTER THIRTEEN

The United Citizens For Law Enforcement

Shortly after the investigative hearings closed, a county-wide steering committee began to search beyond the churches for a strong civic leader who could continue the march toward civil reform. On January 14, the committee met and chose George Dishman as that leader. An oil man, rancher, and president of the South Park Independent District school board, Dishman seemed the perfect choice to lead the newly conceived United Citizens for Law Enforcement, an organization of volunteers from the ranks of the citizenry. The committee also elected Spain Bates of Port Arthur as vice president, J. C. "Huck" Barry of Beaumont, secretary, and Paul L. Robinson of Groves, treasurer. Port Arthur attorney B. T. McWhorter served as attorney for the organization.[1]

The organization stated as its first objective, "the orderly and rational resignations of some public officials," and actively sought the advice of Assistant Attorney General Ben Harrison regarding methods of removing county officials from office.[2] Within the next few years, UNCLE or UCLE, the organization's popular acronyms, would prove to be among the most effective forces to assist in the cleanup of the county.

Many citizens applauded their efforts. However, others interpreted the crusade-like spirit of the organization as the renewal of a type of McCarthyism and feared that the "purging" of the local government would get out of hand. Some groups even formed to counter the efforts of the organization. The Citizens Committee for Democratic Law and Order, led by John Flowers of the Boilermakers Union, criticized UCLE by calling the organization a bunch of "headhunters" who sought to deny constitutional rights of due process to officials suspected of wrongdoing.[3]

Although Harrison promised the support of Attorney General Will Wilson, he reminded members of UCLE that the attorney general's office was "primarily civil, not criminal . . . not a police agency." Harrison also explained that his office would use all laws available to it, especially those it shared with the district attorney, to shut down vice. In addition, he pointed out, if no district judge in Jefferson County was willing to exercise his statutory power to remove the elected officials under fire, the citizenry of Jefferson County themselves could remove those charged with official misconduct, with a jury conviction.[4]

Hoping to expand its membership rolls to include an astounding 50,000 people, UCLE sold membership cards for $1 at central locations throughout the county, conducted a "mother's door-to-door march," co-chaired by Virginia Christopher and Harriott Ivers, and organized a countywide telephone committee, chaired by Mrs. C. O. McNease. The group also incorporated as a nonprofit "educational organization." With its new title and official status, UCLE, Inc. went public with the names of the men it sought to remove from office.[5]

The executive manager of the Ford Motor Company in Dallas and president of the Dallas Crime Commission, John McKee, offered his help to the organization in an advisory capacity, citing the extensive experience he had gained in the cleanup of vice conditions in Dallas. McKee told the executive members of UCLE that he could help them "avoid pitfalls" during their work. The Dallasite prefaced his statements with a warning to the organization against becoming political and urged cooperation with the press saying "[t]he press will stay with you as long as you are factual."[6]

After meeting with Attorney General Wilson, the steering committee of the organization charged ahead to see that the group met its goals. As a first step, the committee developed a ten-point immediate action program, which included as its specific goal the speedy removal of key officials from office. The program adopted by the organization sought to:

1. Establish a daily column in the newspapers under the heading "UNCLE says," devoted to educational information, news and objectives of the UNCLE.
2. Seek VOLUNTARY resignations of key officials by every feasible pressure action.
   a. Have officers of UNCLE prepare and deliver personally and publicize formal requests for the resignations of county, city, and precinct officials in question.
   b. Intensify pressure by having a similar parade of requests from other organizations.
3. Maintain contact with the attorney general's office and the grand jury to establish publicly the desires of UNCLE.
4. Establish a citizen's reporting and complaint system to provide a sounding board where normal channels are not sufficient.
5. Create a small investigative action committee to maintain a realistic appreciation of grass-roots conditions.
6. Promote panel-type question and answer discussions by election candidates before each election.
7. Promote meetings with and secure advice from men who have worked in successful cleanup efforts elsewhere.
8. Expedite citizen's membership card sales preferably through existing organizations.
9. Push for changes in the county grand jury system to permit five instead of three commissioners to pick grand jury members
10. Establish a speakers' bureau to help promote public information and education.[7]

In its first official move, UCLE went after District Attorney Ramie Griffin, apparently because he was seen as the weakest politically and the easiest target. With the help of Assistant Attorneys General Gordon Cass and Vernon Toefan, the reformers petitioned District Judge Harold Clayton to use his statutory powers to begin removal proceedings against the district attorney, citing four instances of official misconduct. Griffin denied all allegations against him, charging that such an unprecedented move by an attorney general to seek the removal of a criminal district attorney was simply a political maneuver by Will Wilson to get some free publicity in Wilson's campaign for the U.S. Senate.[8]

Despite the accusations of political motivations, Judge Clayton temporarily removed Griffin from office and appointed W. G. "Gale" Walley, Jr., as district attorney *pro tem* to assume Griffin's duties while the court heard Griffin's suit. Assistant Attorney General Cass explained to the eager media that Walley would also assume Griffin's power to remove other officials accused of misconduct.[9]

Meanwhile, Quentin Keith and his son Robert, attorneys for Griffin, geared up to defend the embattled district attorney. The Keiths realized that the reformers would be satisfied only when Griffin was removed permanently from office, and subsequently, they laid out a strategy for the difficult work ahead. "But, we felt that Ramie was entitled to fair representation," recalled Robert Keith. "Besides, my father loved the rough and tumble skirmishes a lawyer gets into in courtroom litigation. He was fearless; he reveled in the fight."[10]

The Keiths first tried to stop the removal on jurisdictional grounds, arguing that Clayton's court, a civil court, had no jurisdiction to hear and determine the action against the district attorney, an officer of the Criminal District Court. The State Supreme Court denied the motion.[11]

With the denial of the defense team's motion, Judge Clayton, now given undisputed authority, proceeded with the request to oust Griffin permanently and to suspend him meanwhile. On Wednesday, March 15, Clayton signed the formal order temporarily suspending Griffin. The decision, unprecedented in the state's history, was the beginning of a remarkable chapter in the annals of Texas jurisprudence.[12]

Members of the United Citizens for Law Enforcement came from a broad spectrum of the community, and they chose a highly respected individual to guide them through the legal process necessary to accomplish their goals. To this end, UNCLE followed a dignified and legal process in working toward objectives that would ensure harmony within the community and, at the same time, complete the difficult work ahead.

Texas Attorney General Will Wilson spoke before members of the United Citizens for Law Enforcement in Beaumont on August 22, 1961. Left to right, seated: Acting District Attorney W. G. Walley, Jr., Will Wilson. Standing: J. C. "Huck" Barry, UCLE secretary; George Dishman, UCLE president.

—Photo from *The American Weekly*,
a supplement to the *Houston Chronicle*.
The George Dishman files.
Courtesy James Dishman

District Judge Harold Robert Clayton, known as the quiet and unassuming reform judge who followed the letter of the law, presided over the 136ᵗʰ District Court in the early 1960s.
—Courtesy Kathy McCollum,
court coordinator of the 60th
District Court

Members of the 1962 United Citizens for Law Enforcement Board of Governors. Left to right, seated: Carroll Buttrill, Walter Bush, Mrs. R. L. Wickware, Walter C. Juncker. Standing: J. C. Barry, Spain Bates, Paul Robinson, William Key, Patrick O'Bryan (executive director), George Dishman. Not shown are A. D. Moore, Sr., and the Rev. Dr. John Wright. Photo appeared in the Port Arthur News.

—Courtesy James Dishman

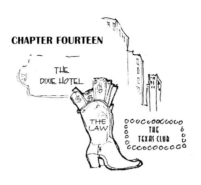

CHAPTER FOURTEEN

The Special Services Vice Squads

The vice squads that formed in Beaumont and Port Arthur on the heels of Jefferson County's greatest upheaval in memory proved to be exceptional crime fighters. Realizing that the officers on the squads would face grueling schedules of intensely dangerous work, the police chiefs in both cities rotated the positions of the officers as quickly as it was feasible. No matter how dedicated an officer was, working under such stressful conditions over an extended period was simply too much for anyone to take.

On January 12, 1961, Beaumont Police Chief Willie Bauer formed the Special Services Detail and assigned Lieutenant Harold C. Walling as head of the division.[1] In October 1961, Bauer promoted Walling to captain, and John Parsons filled his former position. Officer Gene Corder occupied that position next, followed by Cecil Rush and Charles Perricone. During the early '60s, all members of the police force assisted these head officers, along with their detectives. Working closely with the police departments in both cities were the officers of the United Citizens for Law Enforcement, as well as the high officials of such industries as Gulf States Utilities, Dupont, Southwestern Bell, and members of the Ministers' Association.[2]

"We went from gambling to prostitution to the drink joints to the narcotics, and then we'd go back to the gambling," said John Parsons. "One officer said that the reason we were able to discover and bust so many of the vice operations was because the Ministers' Association was praying for us. We met often with [UCLE's] George Dishman and Huck Barry." Parsons described Dishman as a true Christian warrior. He wasn't a big man, but "could imitate the actions of a tiger."[3]

Although the officers of the vice squads were aware of many of the activities within the fields of prostitution and gambling, they soon learned of the growing problem of narcotics in the southeast Texas community. According to Parsons, the suppliers in the area bought the illegal drugs in Mexico, which were mainly barbiturates and amphetamines with street names such as Redbirds, Bluebirds, Yellow Jackets, and Christmas Trees.

Pooling their mental resources, members of the Beaumont Vice Squad planned an effective scheme of detection. They went to the Beaumont city chemist, Bill McClain, and asked him to try to create a "pill" that resembled one of the popular narcotic ones. McClain filled a multitude of capsules with baking soda and caffeine tablets, and an undercover man went to various drug parties in the area, carrying the capsules. At one of the parties, the man reported that everyone dumped their pills into a bowl, and those who "popped the fake pills into their mouths got just as high as a Georgia Pine."

While Parsons found humor in the undercover man's story, he discovered the sad side as well. He learned from some of the young boys that prostitutes had introduced them to drugs and they had become addicts. "The girls thought it was funny," Parsons said.[4]

Vice officer Charles Perricone recalled a time when one man literally decided to cash in on the drug trade by growing marijuana plants at the Castle Motel in Beaumont. After the police department was notified of the man's illegal endeavors, Perricone and his fellow officers dressed in camouflage suits and hid out for days in the bushes around the motel, watching him manicure his plants in every flower box on the premises. "When we had observed enough, we got a search warrant and arrested him," said Perricone. "He was good-natured about the whole thing, though, probably because he was half high."[5]

Special Services director Gene Corder devised a more ingenious plan to stage a raid at a residence on Irving Street, where only black patrons were allowed. The investigating officers knew that Ernest Lombard, a gambling operator under surveillance there, was very familiar with everyone on the police force and could quickly shut his games down when he smelled trouble.

John Parsons, who by then had been promoted to shift captain, and Corder finally devised a plan they felt might work. They decided to contact the theatrical department at Lamar University and have students apply black makeup to the nine officers designated to stage the raid. Successful in their disguise, the officers entered the residence and joined in the game where many players were shooting dice. "When they handed the dice to [Clifford] Baize," said Parsons., "he pulled out his badge and yelled, 'We're police officers and you're under arrest!'" Convinced that his comment was a joke, one of the players yelled back, "Oh, man, cut that B.S. and shoot the dice!" But when the officer reached in his belt, pulled out a revolver, and ordered everyone to line up against the wall, the players realized the raid was real. "Guns, marijuana cigarettes, razors, and everything else hit the floor," said Parsons. "The gamblers in there didn't stand a chance because they had an electromagnet in that table and magnetized dice."

After the officers arrested Lombard and were transporting him to the police station, Parsons remembered him asking, "What the hell ever happened to the old police department? I could have gotten away with this before." But when the officers reminded him that the policies within the department had changed, Lombard answered quite nonchalantly, "I guess there ain't no shame in being busted by the best."

"We did some crazy things in those days," recalled Parsons. "I guess it was a situation where unusual circumstances called for unusual methods."[6]

Beaumont Police officers, holding containers of marijuana plants, pictured with an unidentified man at the Castle Motel in Beaumont. Left to right: Bobby Morton, David Ivey, Clifford Baize, Charles Perricone, Tommy Lawhorn, and Gene Corder.
—Courtesy Charles Perricone

Beaumont police officers as they appeared before staging a raid on Irving Street. Left to right, seated: Norman Boone, Gary Breaux, Clifford Baize, and Gene Wilson. Standing: Harold Engstrom, David Ivey, Gene Corder, John Parsons, and Charles Perricone.
—Courtesy Charles Perricone

CHAPTER FIFTEEN

Ground-breaking Grand Juries and Courthouse Races

The citizens of Jefferson County understood that no matter how many officials city managers fired, the problem would remain unsolved unless responsible members of society took appropriate legal action to punish guilty parties. The only means by which the people of Jefferson County could reclaim their government rested with the members of the January 1961 term grand jury. Editorials filled the *Beaumont Enterprise* and the *Beaumont Journal* that encouraged the incoming grand jurors to realize the responsibility that they faced. "Never has the duty of jurors been so clearly defined," stated one writer. The incoming grand jury had the power to write an entire new chapter on cleanliness in Jefferson County. "Justice demands that it be written."[1]

Given the tradition of grand jury performances in Jefferson County, the situation looked grim. Newspapers and local gossip predicted that grand jurors would return their customary series of no-bills for accused persons and that the recent hearings would go down in history as just another fruitless attempt to salvage a society already defeated by corruption. Sam Landrum, the foreman of the January term grand jury, promised to prove such rumors wrong as he led his team into three months of unprecedented grand jury deliberations.

On its first day, the grand jury heard three witnesses, with Beaumont District Supervisor of the Texas Liquor Control Board El Roy Mauldin the first to testify. Next, local attorney Wyatt Baldwin, who served as legal counsel for Constable Reagan Baker during the committee hearings, answered questions. Casey Revia, a star witness during the hearings, reported he had seen Chief of Detectives Jim Stafford pick up payments at one of the Beaumont clubs. During its first day of official business, the Jefferson County grand jury returned eight indictments and no no-bills.[2]

Meanwhile, as the grand jury was hard at work, Gordon Cass and Ben Harrison, assistant attorneys general sent by Wilson to assist Landrum, were stirring up tempers by their efforts to facilitate the removal of Ramie Griffin as district attorney. Griffin had promised to cooperate with Landrum and the attorney general's office. However, the state did not trust Griffin, who would not surrender quietly the duties of his office to the boys from Austin. Eager to show he was still in control, Griffin had his assistants draw up injunctions against the very clubs he was accused of protecting at the same time the attorney general's office used its injunctive power to stop gambling. The situation escalated, almost comically, into a race to the courthouse between the assistants of Wilson and the assistants of Griffin. At one point, Assistant District Attorneys Jim Vollers and James Farris were preparing an injunction against the Pen Yan Club when they learned that Assistant Attorney General Riley Eugene Fletcher had beaten them to the punch at the 60th District Court. When Farris and Vollers learned of Fletcher's action, they moved quickly to file six more injunction suits against clubs in downtown Beaumont before Fletcher could get to the courthouse.

The injunction race continued with suits against houses of prostitution in Beaumont and Port Arthur. As Jim Farris worked on the third floor of the courthouse drawing up suit papers for Griffin to file against five Beaumont houses, Assistant Attorney General Sam Wilson filed injunctive suits against the very same houses on the second floor. Before he was suspended, however, Griffin succeeded in being first to the courthouse to file against 10 well known brothels in Port Arthur.[3]

The public may have found humor in the methods used to exercise injunctive power against the vice operators in town, but the evidence that backed up the injunctive relief was anything but laughable. In addition to countless reports about gambling, state and district attorneys listened to hours of testimony from local police officers about victims of the vice they sought to enjoin.

John Parsons, the Beaumont vice officer, was one who often testified in private session. Questioning many of the prostitutes after the December 3, 1960, raids, he later related two accounts of torture given by prostitutes he interviewed. "One girl admitted that when she got out of line, her pimp would strip her and beat her with a straightened out coat hanger," Parsons recalled. He noted that she was beaten on her lower back, always in the same place, so it wouldn't "hurt the merchandise." Another prostitute told Parsons how her pimp would put an ice cube "where it would be most uncomfortable" while he was holding her down.[4]

On February 2, 1961, the Jefferson County grand jury returned a series of indictments on felony gambling charges against 20 men, including several of the witnesses who took the Fifth Amendment during the hearings. Sam Siragusa, William Sekaly, and John Graffaganino joined 17 others in racking up indictments for bookmaking, keeping gambling houses, or operating dice or card games at five downtown Beaumont clubs.[5] Later, on March 15, the Jefferson County grand jury turned its attention toward various public officials. It returned 14 indictments, naming Sheriff Charley Meyer; O'Neil Provost, constable of Precinct 2 in Port Arthur; G. B. Graham, constable of Precinct 7 in Groves. It also returned indictments for former Port Arthur Police Chief Garland Douglas on two counts each of accepting bribes from N. H. (Ted) Helms, owner of the Jefferson County Novelty Company. The grand jury likewise indicted Helms on six counts of bribery. All the men named in the indictments denied the charges.[6]

UCLE Vice President Spain Bates filed with the 136th District Court an affidavit in which he identified Helms as a conspirator with the district attorney to allow pinball machines to operate. Bates's affidavit also cited Helms as the man indicted for allegedly bribing Provost, Graham, and Douglas. Attached to the affidavit was an audit that sought to demonstrate Griffin's "unlawful collection of fees." It charged that Griffin "did willfully and unlawfully demand and receive unauthorized fees of office in the sum of $491.74 under the guise of collection fees for collecting dishonored checks presented to him and collected by him in his official capacity as district attorney."[7]

On March 16, the grand jury issued 10 more indictments against Justice of the Peace Lloyd Blanchard of Port Arthur and George Walker, the city marshal of Groves. The indictments charged the men on two counts each for having accepted bribes from Helms. Helms reportedly made the bribes "with the understanding that the officials would not arrest or otherwise interfere with Mr. Helms for unlawfully keeping and exhibiting marble machines for the purpose of gambling." Both men categorically denied all allegations against them.[8] On March 23, Acting District Attorney Walley filed removal suits against Blanchard, Provost, and Graham on behalf of the executive members of UCLE citing "official misconduct and incompetence."[9]

Despite his suspension, Ramie Griffin continued to handle some routine cases with the grand jury, but Judge Clayton excluded him from taking part in the vice investigation. The suspended district attorney charged "politics" and also complained that the UCLE group was "composed primarily of representatives of big business who apparently want to obtain complete control of the county offices."[10]

On March 27, 1961, UCLE officials James Barry and George Dishman petitioned Walley to file a removal suit against Meyer. Walley filed the suit in Judge Gordon Gary's 60th District Court charging the sheriff with "official misconduct and incompetence," and alleging that the sheriff entered into a conspiracy with Helms to permit the unlawful keeping of pinball and marble machines for the purposes of gambling. The grand jurors contemporaneously told Walley that their vice investigation "was being hampered by the sheriff remaining in full command of his office." They had reason to believe, Landrum stated, that Meyer used his official position to intimidate witnesses who were to appear before the grand jury. The sheriff, upon learning of the suit against him, declared "a few are attempting to assume authority over and above the will of the people as expressed at the polls. This is always the beginning of dictatorial rule."[11]

In its final week of duty, the January term grand jury heard testimony from Constable Reagan Baker of Precinct 1. Baker invoked the Fifth Amendment 19 times in 15 minutes before the grand jury after Lord refused to grant him immunity. Baker declined to answer any questions dealing with his knowledge of gambling, bawdy houses, illegal private clubs, and pinball operations. He also refused to comment about any alleged payoffs to officials.[12]

By March 31, the members of the January term grand jury had ended their tenure. They had indicted 11 persons for keeping a gaming house, 14 for bookmaking, and six, including five public officials, for accepting bribes. Mr. Helms received indictments on 12 counts of bribery and five counts for keeping gambling devices. The tireless efforts of the Grand Jury Association in 1960 had laid the foundation for tremendous change; now the work of Barry, Cappel, and Juncker was paying off. Within the memory of Judge Lord, the gambling indictments returned by the January 1961 term grand jury were the first in Jefferson County in 30 years. The outgoing grand jury called upon the April term grand jury to continue the vice probe, and specifically, to launch an investigation into the numbers racket in Jefferson County.[13]

Members of the April term grand jury convened on April 3, 1961, and under the leadership of their foreman, J. M. Fournet, immediately began to carry forth the recommendations of the previous grand jury. In addition to meeting every Thursday to concentrate on what they deemed routine matters, the members met in 13 special sessions to investigate gaming law violations and the numbers racket in Jefferson County.[14] On May 2, the grand jury indicted Don Evans, Jr., Everett Melton Sells, and M. C. "Blue Buddy" Carter on a total of 71 felony gambling indictments. It then followed by returning 81 felony policy game indictments against Eugene DeFretes, James Boyer, and Joel B. Hawkins on May 11. The grand jury returned 27 felony policy game indictments against Herbert Johnson on May 16.[15] As a result of the many hours of lengthy sessions, the April term grand jury returned 284 true bills and 32 no-bills, all of which dealt with illegal gambling.[16]

During the tenure of the April grand jury, the notoriety surrounding Jefferson County grew to nationwide proportions. On May 17, U.S. Attorney General Robert F. Kennedy asked Congress to go after hoodlums and racketeers who "have become so rich and so powerful that they have outgrown local authorities," and specified in his report "the rape of the city of Beaumont by organized crime."[17] Individuals who were foes of the Kennedy administration took issue with Robert Kennedy's reference to Beaumont. They contended that Kennedy made the statement only to weaken the position of Vice President Lyndon Johnson because it showed the corruption that existed within his state. Nevertheless, Kennedy proved to be helpful throughout the cleanup campaign. On June 26, 1961, Assistant U.S. Attorney William G. Hundley appeared before an estimated crowd of 1,800 concerned citizens in the Beaumont City Auditorium and encouraged them to keep up the fight. Hundley called Jefferson County a "model for the rest of the nation."[18]

The growing story of vice and corruption in Jefferson County was mentioned in several state and national publications during the following months. On October 8, 1961, *The American Weekly,* a supplement to *The Houston Chronicle,* featured Beaumont in an article entitled "Corruption of a City."[19] And in the June 12, 1962, issue of *Time,* the sins of the city were portrayed in the article "This Rotten Mess."[20] But the June 1962 issue of *Cavalier,* a magazine that contained the article "Through the Looking Glass with the TALL Americans," caused the loudest outcry, prompting one local distributor, on the advice of his attorney, to keep the magazine off his newsstand. The article, which described white envelopes full of money flying through the air in Jefferson County, coined the name "Honest Charlie" for Sheriff Meyer, and called District Attorney Ramie Griffin "one hell of a gin rummy player," was apparently too much to take.[21] With all the adverse publicity it received, it is little wonder that Beaumont began to be referred to as one of America's "sin cities."

Despite the negative portrayal in the media, real progress was being made by mid-1961 to turn things around in Jefferson County. The credit for this belonged in large part to the hard work of the January and April grand juries. With the help of assistant attorneys general sent from Austin and assistant district attorneys on the local level, the ground-breaking grand juries began what would become a long and seemingly never-ending process toward civic reform.

Drawing from the June, 1962, issue of the Cavalier Magazine, *depicting the payoffs to various public officials.*

Acting District Attorney W. G. Walley, Jr., confers with Sam Landrum, foreman of the January 1961 term grand jury.

—Courtesy the Tyrrell Historical Library

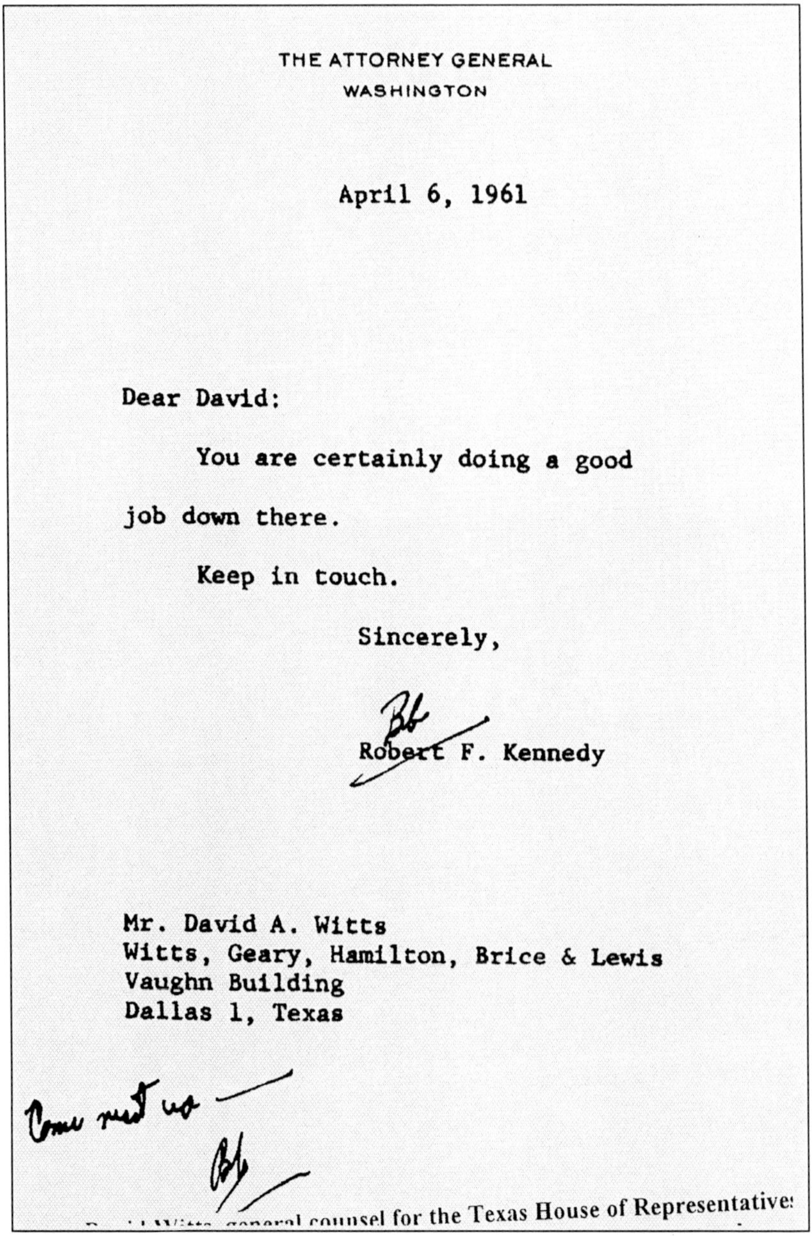

THE ATTORNEY GENERAL
WASHINGTON

April 6, 1961

Dear David:

You are certainly doing a good

job down there.

Keep in touch.

Sincerely,

Robert F. Kennedy

Mr. David A. Witts
Witts, Geary, Hamilton, Brice & Lewis
Vaughn Building
Dallas 1, Texas

Come meet us ——

Bob

counsel for the Texas House of Representatives

According to David Witts, general counsel for the Texas House of Representatives General Investigating Committee, the above letter was the only laudatory correspondence his committee received from U.S. Attorney General Robert Kennedy.

—Courtesy David Witts

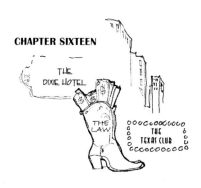

CHAPTER SIXTEEN

Gambling Was Their Way of Life

On July 3, 1961, Judge Owen Lord swore in the new members of the July term Criminal Court Grand Jury, appointing H. M. Nix, Jr., foreman. In his charge to the grand jury, despite the suspicion surrounding him, Lord urged the members to continue the investigation of vice in Jefferson County. He stated that the county provided "a rich field for gambling and prostitution because of the large number of men with money to spend with idle time on their hands, working only 40 hours a week." Branding gambling as "the most demoralizing vice there is," Lord referred to professional gamblers as men who "sit in the shade and air conditioning thinking of ways to beat the working man out of his wages while the working man sweats in the sun." He then stated that he did not believe there was much gambling and prostitution in the county at that time.[1]

Apparently, when Judge Lord addressed the jury he was unaware, or maybe unconcerned, that many of the gambling establishments in downtown Beaumont were back in business. Only five days later, at 1:30 P.M. on July 8, Texas Rangers and 35 Beaumont police officers marched into nine downtown domino clubs and arrested 12 persons, wrapping up two months of undercover work directed by the Special Services Vice Squad. Among those charged with felony bookmaking were Leo Damaris and Raymond Lefkowitz, identified as operators of the Oyster Bar and Lounge, and Joseph Wallent, operator of Fuller's Rooms. Police Chief Willie Bauer reported to the grand jury that he suspected both establishments to be the headquarters of the alleged gambling activities. William C. Sekaly, who only the day before had been sentenced to a two-year probationary term on gambling charges resulting from the raids of December 3, 1960, was also charged. Other clubs identified in the raids were the Bowie Club, Rich's Club, the Texas Club, the Yukon Club, the Commodore Club, the Liberal Club, and Bud's Bar. With the exception of the Oyster Bar, officials had served injunctions against all of them, stemming from raids the December before. Soon thereafter, Judge Harold Clayton issued a temporary restraining order against further operations at the Oyster Bar. Workers immediately began to load equipment and gambling paraphernalia into a moving van. Officials confiscated about $3,200 from the place, along with $1,963 from Damaris and about $850 from Lefkowitz.[2] Two days later, on July 10, police padlocked the Oyster Bar and loaded furnishings into a van from two of Fuller's Rooms and placed them in storage.[3]

Detective John Parsons, who participated in much of the undercover work before the raids, later recalled how police were able to crack the case on the Oyster Bar by sending in an undercover officer dressed in a uniform from Gulf States Utilities. When the IRS later examined the books from the Oyster Bar, one real and one fabricated, it determined that an astonishing amount of money was going out of Beaumont each year on gambling alone.[4]

The Oyster Bar trial, known to be the biggest gambling trial of the vice cleanup campaign, began on January 29, 1962, in Judge Clayton's courtroom.[5] It was a scary time," remembered Parsons. "Because of all the threats I received, a detective from the force was sent to watch my children at school."[6] On February 2, the jury found Leo Demaris guilty of bookmaking and sentenced him to a year in prison. By contrast, the jury ruled in favor of Raymond Lefkowitz, along with two others, and declared them not guilty.[7] Although Demaris's gambling conviction was appealed to the Texas Court of Criminal Appeals, where it was reversed on November 14, 1962, he and Lefkowitz were sentenced on July 29, 1963, to one year in federal prison and fined $750 each for violating the Federal Wagering Act.[8] Most of the area gamblers escaped conviction on the county level, but some joined Demaris and Lefkowitz and later were convicted in federal courts on income tax evasion.

Reminiscing about the year he served in federal prison, Lefkowitz harbored few bad memories: "It was like being in a country club with tennis courts and a golf course." After his release, the gambler admittedly continued to run gambling operations, which he called "sneaking," until the early 1980s. "I was raided along with about 15 others by the FBI in the late 1970s," Lefkowitz recalled. "I was later raided at the Ridgewood [motel] and at a man's apartment." Lefkowitz never looked back on his life with regret. "It was a way of life. It wasn't just for the money. It was for the thrill."[9]

As Lefkowitz continued his gambling pursuits for many years after the Oyster Bar raid, he also managed several restaurants and later became a volunteer for the American Cancer Society. The Society awarded him many honors and one year voted him Volunteer of the Year.[10]

Years after John Parsons retired as a major from the Beaumont Police Department, he recalled, almost with affection, the colorful characters he pursued. "With the exception of a few, most of the gamblers didn't have a harmful bone in their body," he remembered. Walter Sekaly, owner of the Texas Club, was among his favorites. "We'd go in with a warrant and he'd say, 'Yes, my son, how can I help you?'" It was an unwritten code they lived by, Parsons came to realize. "I'll do this or die."[11]

Cartoon drawing from the Beaumont Enterprise *after the July 8, 1961, raids.*

After the Oyster Bar raid on July 8, 1961, workers remove illegal alcohol and gambling paraphernalia into a moving van.

—Courtesy the Tyrrell Historical Library

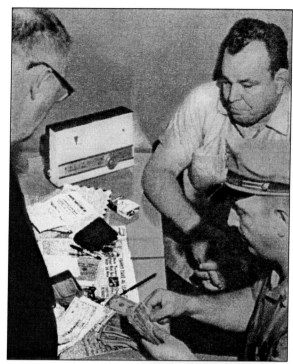

Leo Damaris, top right, operator of the Oyster Bar and Lounge in Beaumont, was charged with felony bookmaking on July 8, 1961.
—Photo from *The American Weekly*, a supplement to *The Houston Chronicle*. The George Dishman files. Courtesy James Dishman

Joseph Wallent, right, operator of Fuller's Rooms, as he appeared with Beaumont Police Officer John Parsons on July 8, 1961.
—Microfilm photo from the *Beaumont Enterprise*. Courtesy the Beaumont Public Library

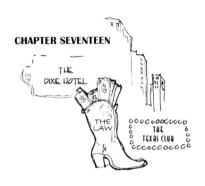

CHAPTER SEVENTEEN

Opposing Tempers
Begin to Flare

As the days of July 1961 quickly progressed, multiple news agencies kept the citizens of southeast Texas, as well as others around the state, well informed of the legal proceedings that were taking place in Jefferson County. The July 8 raids on gambling halls in downtown Beaumont proved to the local operators that police officials had become watchdogs by monitoring their every move. In contrast, the trial seeking the permanent removal of District Attorney Ramie Griffin was not running so smoothly. Griffin's trial, which began on July 12, in Judge Harold Clayton's 136th District Court, contained 25 charges, including that the district attorney:

1. Accepted a bribe from Jack Greer, former operator of the Ritz Dinner Club, to permit Greer to operate the club as an "open saloon."
2. Had knowledge of the operation of gambling establishments in the county but failed to take injunctive actions.
3. Knew of the operation of various houses of prostitution but did not file injunction suits.
4. Charged unauthorized fees for collecting "hot checks" presented to his office by merchants and others.

5. Became intoxicated at a party he hosted for the former grand jurors at the High Island Fishing Pier in October 1960.
6. Failed to post the proper bond at the time he assumed office for his current four-year term.[1]

Immediately after the court was called to order, Acting District Attorney Walley, who was assisted in the trial by Houston attorneys Joe Moss and Fred Hooey, laid the groundwork for lively testimony by calling aloud the names of 60 subpoenaed witnesses, including Rita Ainsworth, Grace Woodyard, and Marcella Chadwell.[2] Griffin's attorneys, Quentin and Robert Keith, had expected Walley to call the madams as witnesses. To their astonishment, however, Assistant District Attorney Creighton Maynard escorted into the courtroom an attractive and well-dressed woman, ex-prostitute Lillian Haager, alias Lee Morris, from New Orleans. Ms. Haager stated that she had previously worked at three houses of prostitution in Beaumont and testified that she had seen Griffin on several occasions having conversations with Rita Ainsworth in her apartment at the Dixie Hotel when Haager was employed there in March of 1958.

Immediately following the woman's testimony, Griffin asked to be called to the stand, where he turned to the jury and raised his right hand emotionally, stating loudly, "I swear to God and hope I'm dead and my two children drop dead if I have ever been in Rita Ainsworth's."[3] The defense team fought hard, and in closing arguments, Quentin Keith left no doubt in the minds of the jurors that leaders in the United Citizens for Law Enforcement were responsible for the accusations made against Griffin. The real issue involved, Keith argued, was "whether we're going to surrender our democratic rights to a self-appointed group who's convinced that only they have the right to say who holds office." Keith also stressed that of the six men who had filed the removal suit, all members of UCLE, J. C. Barry was the only one who had taken the stand during the trial. Keith closed his argument by throwing a copy of the court's charge to the floor and shouting for the jurors to answer all of the issues in Griffin's favor. "Say to these men that you are not going to put this man out of office when they haven't got the guts to come in here and face the accused," he shouted.[4]

The passionate defense team persuaded the majority of the jurors to vote in favor of Griffin's acquittal on all 25 issues. Those jurors opposed to acquittal held firm, and the foreman reported the jury as "hopelessly deadlocked." On July 22 Judge Clayton declared a mistrial.[5]

Griffin's success was short-lived. On July 31, Judge Clayton set off a legal explosion when he granted the state's motion to change the venue of Griffin's new trial to Tyler County. After his shocking ruling, Clayton dropped another bombshell when he revealed that he had been offered a $10,000 bribe to dismiss the Griffin suit altogether and that he was "threatened with physical harm and political ruin" if he did not comply. Acting District Attorney Walley then responded with a statement that he, too, had received threats.[6]

Quentin Keith wasted no time in taking issue with Clayton's actions by saying that his integrity and that of his client were under fire. He filed a document in the Jefferson County district clerk's office on August 1, stating that he could no longer participate in proceedings in Clayton's court. "I will never go inside the rail or sit at the counsel table in that court again," he said. Suspecting that Clayton's allegations were a trumped up effort to circumvent Griffin's right to be tried in Jefferson County, Keith requested that the Jefferson County Bar Association make a "full and complete investigation to determine the truth" of Clayton's charges.[7] Directors of the bar association met immediately in a called, closed-door session but took little action other than to unanimously adopt a resolution in which they condemned the use of any means to exert pressure upon the judiciary.[8]

Although the directors of the bar association ruled against taking sides in the legal controversy, the Citizens for Democratic Law and Order (CDLO) quickly went on the offensive by offering a $1,000 reward for information leading to the arrest and conviction of anyone making threats against either the judge or Walley. The statement also questioned why Judge Clayton had not reported the threatening incidents earlier. "We further believe," said the CDLO, "that the judge's statement was political in nature and was an attempt to throw a smokescreen over his rulings in favor of the state during the change of venue hearing."[9]

In August the CDLO continued to voice its objections to reform efforts through the publication of *The Verdict*, a widely distributed newsletter. In it the CDLO urged the citizens of Jefferson

County to resist being influenced by the political uproar that sought to substitute "the soap box for the jury box.... Let no man be ruled by hysteria, mob rule, preconceived ideas of guilt or other such motives. Let the Democratic process of law and order govern and in the end justice will prevail."[10]

Cartoon drawing from the Beaumont Enterprise *after the Jefferson County Bar Association adopted a resolution in July 1961 condemning the use of pressure upon the judiciary.*

Ramie Griffin, left, pictured with his attorney, Quentin Keith, at Griffin's trial on July 12, 1961.
—Courtesy the Tyrrell Historical Library

Courtrrom scene at the Ramie Griffin trial. foreground, left to right: Bob Keith, Ramie Griffin, Quentin Keith, Fred Hooey, Joe Moss, and W. G. Walley, Jr., standing.
—Courtesy the Tyrrell Historical Library

Lillian Haager, alias Lee Morris, at the trial of Ramie Griffin as she was escorted into the 136ᵗʰ District Court by Assistant District Attorney Creighton Maynard.
—Courtesy the Tyrrell
Historical Library

Alleged madams Dorothy McCarty, left, and Mrs. Cecil Honey prictured at the Ramie Griffin trial.
—Courtesy the Tyrrell Historical Library

Jack Greer, as he appeared at the Ramie Griffin trial.
—Courtesy the Tyrrell
Historical Library

Newsletter published in August 1961 by the Citizens for Democratic Law and Order.
—Courtesy James Dishman, from the George Dishman files

CHAPTER EIGHTEEN

Lord vs. Clayton–
"Tabloid Jurisprudence"

By the end of September 1961, the events of the summer, including the mistrial of Ramie Griffin, had sharply divided the community. One side, fueled by members of UCLE, pushed for the removal and prosecution of anyone implicated by the investigation.
The other side was composed of those who believed that crusaders
were about to take over their entire local government and feared for
their civil rights. The Citizens for Democratic Law and Order
(CDLO) voiced the particular concerns of this group. Judge
Clayton found himself thrown into the middle of a political
firestorm that would eventually dissolve into allegations of sexual
impropriety, libel, and slander.

Judge Owen Lord thus far had escaped scrutiny. He continued
to preside over the Criminal District Court although his association
with Griffin and Meyer clearly implicated him in the vice scandal.
Lord had impaneled the January, April, and July term grand juries
which had begun the monumental and groundbreaking task of
tackling the vice problem and handing out indictments against any
official accused of misconduct. But despite Lord's apparent cooperation with the history-making grand juries, key players in the reform movement, most notably members of UCLE, wanted him re-

moved from any proceeding that involved allegations of official misconduct, particularly that of Griffin or Meyer. To best accomplish their mission, UCLE needed to have Judge Clayton, not Lord, impanel a grand jury that would consider charges against the principal players in the old regime. So, on September 18, Judge Clayton named a commission to select a grand jury panel for the October term.[1]

Several days later, just before their tenure ended, five members of the July term grand jury presented a special report to Lord. In it, they accused Acting District Attorney Walley of protecting "those who are claiming to be leaders in the fight for clean government but who, actually are disregarding evidence of heinous lewd sexual offenses and attempted offenses."[2] Another member later joined three of the original signers in issuing a second statement. In their report, they called Judge Clayton's move to impanel a second grand jury "a direct affront to the undersigned, and to all grand jurors who serve with us."[3]

Judge Clayton and jury foreman H. M. Nix, Jr., took issue with the allegations made by members of the July term grand jury and both responded publicly to the criticism contained in the grand jury's reports. In Clayton's statement to the press, he claimed that he had every legal right to impanel a second grand jury and that he did so only in response to the overwhelming workload previous grand juries had faced with the vice investigation. "I am still amazed why my selection of a grand jury panel is of so much concern to such a small group of people . . ."[4] Nix wrote a letter to the district attorney's office in an attempt to further deflect suspicion that the proceedings he had presided over during the last three months were tainted by the prevailing political winds. In doing so, he revealed that his grand jury had considered charges against Judge Clayton's 21-year-old son for lewd activities, a fact Nix did not want to disclose. The jury had returned a no-bill and did not indict the younger Clayton.[5]

On September 29, Judge Owen Lord stood before members of the October term grand jury to swear them in as he had done in years past. On the same day, for the first time in Jefferson County history, Judge Clayton impaneled a second grand jury.[6] He did so in fear that Lord's grand jury would revisit the allegations against his son. Unfortunately, his fears were well founded; while Clayton's grand jury was busy hearing charges stemming from the vice investigation, Lord's grand jury made the case against Clayton's son one of the focal points of its proceedings.

On the morning of September 29, 1961, with the impaneling ceremonies over, both Judge Lord and Judge Clayton instructed their new October term grand jurors. The two adversaries immediately squared off for battle. Combat ensued that very afternoon when local attorney Fred A. Carver filed two "challenges to the array" suits, each of which objected to the legality of Clayton's grand jury. The two suits, filed in Clayton's court, were quickly dismissed by the judge. He defended his actions by contending that under the state constitution any district judge had the right to impanel a grand jury. He further insisted that a second grand jury would help with the workload, since each prior grand jury had been unable to complete its investigation into vice in the county.[7] Citizens within the legal community still look upon the conflict between the two October 1961 term grand juries as one of the most embittered courthouse struggles ever staged in Jefferson County.

Although the leaders of UCLE claimed that their organization was nonpartisan, on October 1 they issued a statement to the *Beaumont Enterprise* in which they praised the actions of Judge Clayton to impanel the second grand jury and questioned the "objectiveness" with which some members of Judge Lord's new jury might approach their duties. The statement contended that several persons serving on Lord's jury had also signed an earlier petition presented to Judge Gary objecting to the removal of Sheriff Meyer from office.[8] In spite of protests, Clayton's grand jury issued a second indictment against Sheriff Meyer. Accusing the sheriff of "false swearing" concerning contributions he had received for his reelection campaign in 1960, the charge indicated that while "in truth and fact" he received $23,870 in gifts and money, he reported only $2,160 in gifts and loans. In addition, the indictment pointed out that Meyer ran unopposed in both the primary and general elections in that year.[9]

One hour after his indictment was handed down, the sheriff issued a statement charging he was the victim of a planned campaign of "harassment," and again questioned the legality of Clayton's jury. "Technicalities are now being perpetuated," Meyer alleged, "and serious crimes ignored by a grand jury chosen under doubtful legal conditions." But the sheriff still found it within himself to wax poetic about the entire situation: "The mountain has labored and brought forth a mouse—it is a real first class fuzzy rat."[10] Two days later, Meyer's attorney, Gilbert Adams, Sr., filed an application for a *writ of habeas corpus* with Judge Lord to get Meyer out of Judge Clayton's court.[11] From there, both sides threw down the gauntlet and the legal proceedings dissolved into an all-out dogfight.

In answer to Adams' application, Walley went before Judge Lord on November 10 and insisted that Judge Lord transfer Meyer's hearing back to Clayton's court. Judge Lord immediately denied his request. In retort, Judge Clayton issued a restraining order that stopped Lord from hearing Meyer's case. On November 20, the Court of Criminal Appeals upheld the order. From there, Meyer's attorney marched into the Texas Supreme Court. On November 29 the high court of Texas reviewed the case with supporting briefs filed by 21 Jefferson County attorneys, all backing Judge Clayton.[12]

While the Texas Supreme Court mulled over the resolution to Jefferson County's jurisdictional quagmire, Lord's grand jury fired a parting shot on November 30 by indicting Judge Clayton's 21-year-old son, Harold Robert Clayton, Jr., on the charge of unlawfully exposing himself to an 11-year-old Groves girl.[13]

This time, Judge Clayton cried politics. On the day of the indictment, Clayton read a personal statement he prepared in which he strongly denied his son's guilt and claimed he was being blackmailed. He further stated that officers accused his son of the criminal offense as soon as he made public his plans to select a second grand jury. Clayton also claimed he had received several ominous "suggestions" encouraging him not to impanel the grand jury. After he proceeded with the impaneling, Clayton insisted he became the target of "scandal sheets" circulated by "people who have been engaged over many years in the gambling profession."[14]

Following the indictment of Judge Clayton's son, both judges suddenly dismissed their grand jurors.[15] Surprised by their dismissal and suspicious of the reason, 11 of the 12 members from Lord's grand jury breached their vows of secrecy and unleashed another sexual scandal. The 11 members issued a statement to the press that appeared in the *Beaumont Enterprise* on December 12, 1961. This time they accused Acting District Attorney Walley of "unlawfully encouraging and contributing to the delinquency" of a minor girl. Outraged, Walley filed a libel suit against the 11 grand jury members and issued his own statement claiming the jurors acted in concert to maliciously circulate and deliver false and defamatory information.[16]

Not a moment too soon, the Texas Supreme Court effectively halted the jurisdictional squabbling in the Jefferson County courts on December 13, when it ruled that Judge Clayton, and any other district judge, had the right to impanel a grand jury. The court also ruled Judge Lord could proceed with the habeas corpus hearing sought by Sheriff Meyer. With clarity from the state's highest court, Clayton and Lord reassembled their grand juries on December 14.[17] Immediately, Lord's grand jury handed down an indictment against Walley for alleged immoral behavior with an underage girl.[18]

In turn, on the same day, Clayton's grand jury began a probe of Lord's grand jury. It investigated, among other things, whether Lord had followed the laws of Texas or selected grand jury members in Lord's "traditional manner," given that its members had expressed their sympathy for Meyer in a letter to Judge Gary. The following day, Clayton's grand jury issued separate indictments against the 11 members of Lord's grand jury who had released details of their proceedings to the press, charging each with unlawfully divulging grand jury proceedings.[19] Since the 11 indictments were misdemeanor cases, Clayton transferred the cases to the County Court-at-Law on December 19, stating that a district court did not have jurisdiction over misdemeanor cases.[20]

Once Clayton moved the indictments, Walley dismissed the libel suit he had filed against the 11 jurors. However, he renewed his claims against the jurors and the Texas Gold Coast Television, Inc., in another civil suit on December 20. Contending that the station had broadcast the grand jury report, he asked for $100,000 in damages. He then filed a second suit asking for $50,000 in damages from the five members who signed a report that he stated had hurt him professionally.[21]

As the two grand juries neared the end of their terms, the legal battle showed no signs of letting up. On December 28, Walley filed a second motion in Judge Gordon Gary's 60th District Court to have Sheriff Meyer suspended from office. Not eager to be in the center of the storm, Judge Gary postponed the hearing to an undetermined date.[22]

With time running out, Lord's grand jury quickly issued subpoenas on December 29, not only to the plaintiffs in the removal suit of Meyer, but also to Judge Clayton and to all members of his grand jury, ordering them to appear before Lord's grand jury the next day.[23] As Lord's officers served the subpoenas, members of Judge Clayton's grand jury already had filed their final report. In it, the jurors stated, "We have been exposed during our investigations to moral corruption of such magnitude as this honorable court has no conception." They alleged, among other things, "theft by persons in high places," for which there are "no legal penalties."[24]

Later on December 29, after Judge Clayton failed to respond to the subpoena, Lord's grand jury ordered Sheriff Meyer to "attach" Judge Clayton and bring him before them. Sensing the situation might get out of hand, Judge Lord ordered Sheriff Meyer and Assistant District Attorney Creighton Maynard to request the assistance of two Texas Rangers. Despite this, Judge Clayton refused to comply, calling the attachment order illegal.[25] As a final affront to Judge Clayton, Judge Lord ordered him to appear in his court on January 10, 1962, on a contempt charge. As the end of the October term neared, however, Judge Lord appeared weary of the in-fighting and ready for a holiday break. He refused repeated requests by his grand jury members to extend their terms. The grand jurors left the courtroom in apparent frustration, knowing that Lord probably would not follow through with the actions they initiated.[26]

Clayton still could not claim victory until his contempt hearing on January 10, 1962. On that morning, people filled the Criminal District courtroom to capacity and spectators lined the halls trying to get in. Judge A. R. Stout, a visiting judge from Waxahachie, presided at the hearing. The court procedure began when Walley declined to present any charges against Judge Clayton. Judge Stout then asked if any Jefferson County lawyer was present to bring the charges. No one stepped forward. Finally, Hardin County attorney Stanley Coe broke the silence and read the contempt charges against Judge Clayton. No stranger to the controversy, Coe had represented Lord's October term grand jury after it was indicted by Clayton's grand jury.

In response to the charges read by Coe, 78 Jefferson County attorneys, led by H. P. Robichau, Jr., and Bar President David Kreager, stood up with Judge Clayton. The group presented a petition in which they asked Judge Stout to dismiss the case against Clayton. After reading the petition and asking a few brief questions, Judge Stout did just that. His ruling caused a roar of cheers throughout the courtroom.[27]

The public did not respond with the same level of enthusiasm. Letters to the editor consistently voiced suspicion that the actions of Clayton in forming a second grand jury were an effort to usurp the power of their locally elected officials. "Why did it suddenly become necessary for a second grand jury to be impaneled by Judge Clayton?" asked Ora Lee Gonzales.[28] But others, such as C. B. Moore, insisted that Clayton's actions were honorable and came to his defense. "Judge Clayton is fighting to clean up the county of the filth of the underworld so that future generations will not have the present conditions to contend with."[29]

Despite the courtroom drama, during the latter part of 1961 the cleanup effort on the streets of Jefferson County made astounding strides. In Beaumont alone, beginning with the formation of the Special Services vice squad on January 12, police conducted nearly 1,500 vice investigations, resulting in 506 arrests. Sixty-six persons were arrested for prostitution, along with 87 for narcotics, 174 for liquor law violations, 13 for felony gambling, 86 for misdemeanor gambling, and 76 for miscellaneous vice offenses.[30]

But, as Beaumont Police Chief Willie Bauer acknowledged in an article in the *Enterprise* on December 31, many of the prostitutes and the men who solicited business for them had not left town. "Although the results of our anti-vice campaign may look impressive, our job is by no means finished," he said. "In fact, it becomes more difficult as time goes by because of underground operations." He vowed, however, that the roundup would continue.[31]

The Texas Supreme Court and its interpretation of law related to impaneling grand juries finally brought the legal maneuvers of the two judges, with their charges and counter charges, under control. Once again, it was time to put animosities aside, to accept judgments from the bench, and to move forward in the cleanup of Jefferson County.

H. M. Nix, Jr., served as foreman of the July 1961 Jefferson County Criminal District Court Grand Jury.

—Courtesy H. M. Nix, Jr.

H. H. "Country" Reynolds (right), a member of the October 1961 Criminal District Court Grand Jury, raises his hands as he protests the refusal by Judge Owen M. Lord to accept two indictments that the grand jury attempted to return. Standing beside Reynolds is C. A. "Red" Kiker, another member of the grand jury.

—Microfilm photo from the *Beaumont Enterprise.*
Courtesy the Beaumont Public Library

PART VI

Turning Over
The Courthouse Keys

CHAPTER NINETEEN

A Changing of the Guard

When William "Bill" Hataway, a Beaumont petroleum engineer and marine chemist, was summoned in late December 1961 to serve on Judge Clayton's January 1962 term grand jury, he couldn't help but be apprehensive. The dust had not yet settled from the legal shoot-out between the previous two juries. Hataway believed that he didn't have the time or the inclination to become embroiled in another drawn-out legal controversy. After all, he had recently started his own business, which involved signing work certificates at Bethlehem Steel for pipe fitters, some of whom were openly critical of Clayton's grand jury. "If a man was killed in an accident or a ship blew up, it could reflect on me," Hataway said. "I didn't think anybody would want to do anything to Bethlehem Steel, but I felt that maybe if they thought they could get to me through Bethlehem, they might do something. For that reason, I knew Judge Clayton would excuse me."

With the expectation that Clayton would honor his request, he approached the judge. However, Clayton refused his request and told the reluctant businessman, "You have time." On January 1, 1962, Hataway appeared with 11 others as Judge Clayton impaneled the jury. Today he recalls that his grand jury tenure was one of the most rewarding experiences of his life.[1]

Contrary to the battle between the two previous grand juries,

Clayton's 136th District Court and Lord's Criminal District Court grand juries vowed to work in harmony. Clayton's jury members focused primarily on continuing the cleanup efforts in the county, while Lord's jurors concentrated on the multitude of pending criminal cases.[2] Citizens and elected officials alike turned their focus from the grand jury circus to the state and county elections scheduled for May 5, 1962.[3]

As new candidates lined up to oppose the incumbents, it soon became apparent that three of the prominent political figures within the ring of controversy were tired of the fight. By the end of February, both Judge Owen Lord and Acting District Attorney Walley had announced that they were choosing not to run. On March 2, District Attorney Ramie Griffin offered his resignation to Governor Price Daniel, stating, "I do so with a clear and convincing feeling that I have been wrongfully accused.

> In submitting my resignation, I do so without hatred in my heart for anyone. My decision comes despite the pleas of hundreds of my friends to continue the fight since they know that I am innocent of the charges. But, to continue fighting when confronted with the personal problems I now have, would serve only to keep alive the struggle for political power now going on in our county.
>
> I am hopeful that my resignation will help cause the strife and turmoil in our county to subside.[4]

When the votes were counted after the May 5 election, it was obvious that the pendulum of justice in Jefferson County had swung to the side of reform. Winning challengers who stood firm on a cleanup platform were Chester Young, who defeated County Judge James A. Kirkland; Cecil Holstead, winning over District Clerk L. R. "Speedy" Blakeman; W. C. Lindsey, who opposed Bill Lea for the soon-to-be vacated district attorney position; and George Taylor, who won after a runoff with Edgar Berlin for Lord's Criminal District Court bench.[5]

Newly elected officials cleared the courthouse of the old regime, yet Sheriff Charley Meyer remained defiant. Facing even more indictments from Clayton's grand jury in January and February 1962, Meyer, nevertheless, continued to fight for his job.[6] He did not face an election year in 1962, but the reformers were still determined to see him out of office. On May 21, 1962, the acting district attorney dropped his removal suit against Meyer. Walley's dismissal effectively removed Meyer's case from Judge Gordon Gary's 60th District Court, where it had languished for more than a year, because Gary had never set it for hearing. Hoping to get things rolling, Walley re-filed his removal suit in Judge Clayton's 136th District Court, which visiting Judge Connally McKay now occupied. Judge McKay granted Walley's petition and suspended Sheriff Meyer. He also named R. E. "Dick" Culbertson, a former member of the State Highway Patrol, to the job of acting sheriff. But again, Meyer proved intransigent and appealed McKay's suspension. Further, he protested the removal of his case from Judge Gary's court and took that issue all the way to the Texas Supreme Court. The high court intervened once more to calm the waters at the Jefferson County courthouse, when it ruled against Meyer and in favor of McKay. Finally, on July 3, 1962, "Dick" Culbertson took over as acting sheriff of Jefferson County.[7]

The Texas Supreme Court suspended Charley Meyer from office, but Charley, though ousted, did not quietly exit the political arena. During the following months, his attorney, Gilbert Adams, took every legal avenue available to prevent his permanent removal. On March 26, 1963, the trial to oust Meyer from office began in the 60th District Court before another visiting judge, Wilmer B. Hunt of Houston. Walley acted as special counsel for the state.

In spite of the multitude of damaging testimony presented against Meyer throughout the trial, Adams maintained in his closing argument that Meyer was "one of the finest men I know."[8] The continuing popularity of the colorful sheriff proved to be a powerful obstacle to the reform movement. On April 5, the jury reported to Judge Hunt that it was hopelessly deadlocked, and the judge declared a mistrial.[9]

Considering the trial a victory, Adams fought to reinstate Meyer as sheriff. On September 6, 1963, in a hearing before the Texas Court of Civil Appeals, Adams presented a request to reinstate Meyer as sheriff of Jefferson County. During the hearing, Adams again glorified his client by calling him "Sir Galahad." This time, however, Walley countered Adams' rhetorical compliment by referring to Meyer as "that errant knight."[10] On October 3, 1963, the appeals court refused to order the reinstatement of Meyer.[11]

Suspension from office did not disqualify Meyer from running again for sheriff. In January 1964, he announced his candidacy against Culbertson, and with the help of his cohorts, orchestrated one of the most aggressive campaigns ever waged in the history of Jefferson County.

Jo Culbertson, who actively campaigned with her husband, recalled that the union workers were 75 percent in favor of Meyer. Many of the workers spit on the campaign materials they passed out at the refinery gates. Mrs. Culbertson decided to appeal to the workers' wives and organized coffees where she and other campaign workers spoke about the county's need for a new sheriff.[12]

Besides the union workers, Dick Culbertson remembered that he also had to contend with a disloyal band of junior deputies, who were sympathetic to their former boss. "They would gather up as many of my cards in front of my headquarters and throw them away and pass out [Meyer's] cards in front of my campaign office in Port Arthur." But the biggest surprise Culbertson received was right before the election, when several of the deputies walked into his office and handed him their letters of resignation. The disgruntled deputies brought the news media along to record Culbertson's reaction as he read their resignation letters. Culbertson simply looked at them and wadded up their letters. Some of the reporters tried to get the letters but Culbertson prevented them from doing so. Eventually, he fired the deputies who were sympathetic to the other side. The newspapers at first were reluctant to endorse Culbertson; but when the refineries threatened to take their money out of local banks and put it in other cities, the newspapers came around, and Culbertson got the endorsement.[13]

On May 2, Dick Culbertson stopped Meyer's ride up the political comeback trail by winning a majority of 5,900 votes in the Democratic primary. With Jefferson County's reputation as a democratic stronghold, Culbertson's win was tantamount to victory in the general election that November.[14] Culbertson's victory heralded the final curtain call for the political players of the old regime. The county was now back to a one grand jury system. With new leaders in key political roles in the county drama, it was time to move forward.

Suspended Sheriff Charley Meyer (left) pictured with his attorney, Gilbert Adams, Sr., at Meyer's ouster from office trial in the 60th District Court in 1963.

—Microfilm photo from the *Beaumont Enterprise.*
Courtesy the Beaumont Public Library

R. E. "Dick" Culbertson (right) as he was sworn in as sheriff of Jefferson County in January 1965 by attorney H. P. Robichau.

—Former Jefferson County Sheriff
R. E. "Dick" Culbertson papers, ms. 175.
Courtesy the Tyrrell Historical Library

PART VII

"Doing What Comes Naturally"

CHAPTER TWENTY

"Birds Do It, Bees Do It, Even Educated Fleas Do It"

Shortly after the Texas House of Representatives General Investigating Committee left Jefferson County in January 1961, Dr. C. L. Pentecost, one of Rita Ainsworth's doctors, attended a medical conference at the Baptist Hospital in Beaumont. As he and the other doctors entered the conference room, they noticed a pretty girl sitting in a chair on the stage, partially covered with a sheet. The doctors could see enough of her skin to realize that her body was covered with sores.

The meeting began with Dr. Bill Smith, the leader of the conference, questioning the girl. "What do you do for a living?" the doctor asked. "I hustle," the girl answered. As the questioning continued, the girl readily admitted that she "worked" the area near the Port of Beaumont, often seeing as many as 12 to 15 men on a weekend.

Dr. Smith then turned to the audience and announced that the girl had the very transmittable disease of secondary syphilis. "One hour in the bed with her and you're well exposed," the doctor said. "Now you can see that we're exporting it all over the world." The conference confirmed what Dr. Pentecost already knew—no laws would ever stop the world's oldest profession. If one should believe otherwise, Pentecost said, he only needed to drive down College Street in Beaumont to see the "girls swinging their purses and swinging their hips." Dr. Pentecost believed that the medical profession and law enforcement officials had a duty to bring prostitution under control.[1]

In Jefferson County, most of the "girls" and madams who ran the infamous brothels had either left the state or scattered into surrounding neighborhoods and towns. With the IRS and the local law enforcing administrations now hot on their trails, the working girls had to be very discreet.

It took only a few days after the Texas Investigating Committee hearings for an article to appear in the *Houston Chronicle* entitled "Stay Out of Orange, Vice Characters Told." The article claimed policemen in Orange had served notice to gamblers and prostitutes to get out of Orange within 24 hours.[2] And, according to former Silsbee City Councilman Pete Landolt, vice operators quickly established themselves in his small East Texas town before the city fathers shut them down. "The interesting thing about it was that they operated right across the street from the Baptist Church," said Landolt, "and there were so many cars there that the people going to church couldn't find a parking place."[3]

Bob Henderson collected back taxes for the IRS from 1962-1966. He recalled that many of the local vice operators couldn't afford to pay their taxes because of the large legal fees they paid to their attorneys during the state investigation. "Once we held an auction at one of the houses after the owner failed to pay the taxes," Henderson said, "and the housewives showed up in droves and almost fought over everything. They bought towels, sheets, pillowcases, mattresses and beds, bidding much higher than they were worth. We got a fortune out of that place. It was hilarious."

Henderson remembered another incident that wasn't quite as funny. His superior officer assigned him and another agent to question a madam who was allegedly operating openly out of a house on Thomas Road, one of the most prestigious residential areas in Beaumont. According to Henderson, the woman previously had been a madam at a downtown hotel and had married into one of the wealthiest families in town. The marriage soon ended in divorce because she failed to meet the approval of her husband's family members, but not before the woman enjoyed a taste of the "good life." She apparently decided to lease a house in an area where she could easily cater to a "blue-blood" clientele. Henderson and another IRS officer went to the woman's house one day to question her about her taxes. Soon after ringing the doorbell, they were startled to turn and see her driving toward them in her Buick. Realizing that she intended to run over them, the officers headed for the front ditch, dodging her car all the way. "Finally, she drove the Buick into the ditch, and that stopped her," Henderson said. "We shut her down there, and she went into operating a little beer joint." In spite of her troubles with the IRS, Henderson recalled that she always lived in lovely homes, drove beautiful cars, and took nice trips. "But we could never find any assets. When we questioned her, she'd say, 'I live off the generosity of my friends.' She got away scot-free."[4]

In the early part of 1963, the Beaumont Police Department began receiving various reports that Rita Ainsworth had gone back into business at her former location at 238½ Crockett. She simply changed the letters on her sign out front from the Dixie Hotel to the Annex Apartments. Vice officers Cecil Rush and Charles Perricone recalled that the department's first tip came from the American Social Hygiene Association. "After we got this report from them, we started watching," said Rush. "But we couldn't get anyone in there. Even a person who had been a good customer couldn't bring a friend in. We had a seaman go there, but he was turned away. We watched it for months."[5]

The officers knew that the police department needed to establish "probable cause" before they could make an arrest. Officers John Parsons and Gene Corder then devised what they thought would be an ingenious plan. They decided to dress like winos and lie out in the alley behind Rita's place to observe who was entering. "We filled Thunderbird jugs with water and dressed in ragged clothes and laid by the back door to get a good look," said Corder. Finally, the department discovered that one of Rita's former prostitutes, who was a known narcotics addict, was living there. After they secured a narcotics search warrant, the vice officers, along with other members of the police department and several members from the sheriff's department and DA's office, were able to enter.

Corder recalled that one group of officers stationed themselves at the back entrance as he and others advanced up the front steps.

What they didn't realize was that when they hit the fourth step, a buzzer sounded within the brothel, alerting Rita that the officers were approaching. Rita locked the door and refused to allow them entrance. Three of the officers began to use sledge hammers in an attempt to beat in the huge steel door. Finally, a deputy who weighed about 300 pounds had to beat the frame out of the wall. After the officers entered, Corder immediately approached the defiant madam and asked, "Rita, where are the whores?" She answered, "What are you talking about? I'm sorry, we don't have any girls up here." Soon, however, the officers stationed in the back alley entered with two of the girls who had attempted to leave through the back door. "Then we heard Rita's maid crying," said Corder. "She was on her knees holding Pat Hayes, the investigator for the DA's office, and begging him not to send her to the penitentiary."[6]

Amid the hysteria of the evening, a drunk came through the opening once covered by the steel door. In his inebriated state he had not heard the officers tear out the door. The officers remembered that he was followed by Rita's attorney, Joe Goodwin, who, according to John Parsons, "ranted and raved about property damage. He came up and got in my face and I said, 'Joe, you got two choices, partner. You can get out of here or you can get the hell out of here.'" Realizing that he would have to take other measures, Goodwin went directly to the Beaumont police station and complained to Police Chief Willie Bauer. "That conversation was shorter than the one I had with him," continued Parsons. "When he came out, I said, 'You can tell Rita to shut it down and leave it down or we will be there again.'"[7]

Police officers arrested Rita and the girls, and officers Corder and Perricone accompanied them to the police station, where they were booked. On the way to the police station, Perricone asked, "Rita, when are you going to quit this business?" She answered, "Let me tell you something, son. I deal in a product that's always in demand and never wears out."[8]

After the arrests, several officers remained to search for drugs. While no drugs were found, one closet contained a cache of pornographic material, which was confiscated and taken to the district attorney's office. Assistant District Attorneys James Farris and Terry Doyle recalled that they were amazed at the assortment of "toys" laying on Investigator Cliff Everett's desk the following Monday morning. "I never will forget," Doyle said. "There was a whip, and the handle of the whip was the leg of a deer. The whip came off with eight or nine tails. It was one of the tools of the trade." While questioning one of the prostitutes later, Doyle again was surprised to learn that one of Rita's regular customers went there only to have stick pins stuck into various parts of his anatomy below his navel and above his knees.[9]

Although it was reported that Rita never operated again at 238½ Crockett, she continued to conduct business on the sly, mainly at her residence at 5035 Concord Road and on East Lucas, at the former home of her good friend Jake Giles. "Every time Rita moved and opened up again," recalled John Parsons, "I'd get a call from a doctor's wife. When her husband's cohorts came to town, they'd go partying and they'd end up at Miss Rita's. Whoever it was that coined the phrase, 'Hell hath no fury like that of a woman scorned' knew exactly what he was talking about, because she burned her [Rita] every time she landed."[10]

In November 1968 the Beaumont Police Department received enough information from the American Social Hygiene Association on the Lucas house to conduct another raid. According to Gene Corder, on the evening of November 28, an undercover man, who had left word with a cab driver, went in first. "We got the code from the driver and gave the man about 15 minutes before we went in," said Corder.

The officers approached the house, Corder recalled, and a bunch of dogs greeted them. "The only bad one in the bunch was a little toy poodle, and I think he bit everybody on the vice squad," he said. The officers went inside and found their undercover man half undressed. The girl who had been "entertaining" him had suddenly disappeared. The officers searched the house, and finally located the missing girl. Rita had stuffed her in a linen closet over the bathtub. "I went in," continued Corder, "and looked her right in the face, and said, 'You sweet thing, I don't know what we'd done without you.' After we got her down, she said, 'It was about time you found me. I was about to smother.'"[11]

On the way over to the police station, Officer Perricone again asked, "Rita, how much longer are you going to do this? You don't need the money." Once again, she answered quite flippantly,

"Perricone, I've been doing this all my life, and I'm going to keep on doing it."[12]

However, the November 1968 incident was the last reported raid of Rita Ainsworth. Like many of the other vice operators in the area, she was forced to sell her real estate and her north-end home after the IRS made her pay $100,000 in taxes for undeclared revenue.[13] She sold the building that housed the Dixie Hotel to Gulf States Utilities on January 24, 1977. Gulf States donated the building on August 8, 1980, to the Beaumont Heritage Society,[14] and today it is part of the popular and lively Crockett Street Entertainment District. Eventually Rita moved to her stepdaughter's home in Deer Park, Texas. Mary Lou cared for her during her declining years and until her death on September 23, 1978.[15]

The death of Rita Ainsworth seemed to send a surreptitious signal to other law violators to step up to the home plate. In the late 1970s a seedy prostitution and drug operation broke out on Forsythe Street in Beaumont. A unit of police, led by Beaumont Police Detective Charles W. "Chuck" Little, mounted a persistent surveillance, and only then were the activities halted.[16]

But, judging from a story told by Attorney Terry Doyle, the oldest profession on earth has remained alive and well. After leaving the district attorney's office, Doyle entered private practice in Port Arthur, where several years ago he represented an older prostitute on a heroin case. "When I represented her, she was servicing the old men on Social Security," said Doyle. "She would go to their houses and entertain them, one in the morning and one in the afternoon."

After about six months, Doyle succeeded in having her case dismissed and met with her at his office. "When she came in, I asked her how she was doing," said Doyle:

> She told me that she had married, and she couldn't believe that sex could be so much fun. "I'm having a ball," she said. "I feel like I'm eighteen years old again." It was hard for me to think that here was a woman that had sex thirty times a month with thirty different guys and she was saying that. I looked at her and asked, "It's never been fun?"
>
> There was a will on top of my desk and it was turned over. "Is that a will?" she asked. I answered, "Yeah." She asked again, "Did you 'get off' when you wrote that will?" I said, "No, I just

wrote the will." Then she smiled and said, "It's the same thing with me."[17]

With the onset of the so-called "sexual revolution" in the '60s, standards that had governed sexual behavior since the Victorian era became more relaxed. In a lifestyle exemplified in the Broadway musicals *Hair* and *Oh, Calcutta*, many young people truly did "what comes naturally." On the other hand, prostitutes who performed for a fee changed not at all. The madams, now closely watched by both the IRS and law officers, found different venues to escape detection. They never exhausted the supply of girls available for hire or of prospective clients. Had a madam practiced pop psychology to unmask her true self, upon discovery she would have said, "I am what I am" and continued in the business. In her self-honesty, she also would have supported another truth: "Men are men, and a goodly number of them will buy what I and my girls have to sell." History, the long, long history from primitive times to the present, supports both these contentions.

Beaumont Police Detective Charles W. "Chuck" Little, forefront, led in the arrests of a prostitution and drug operation of Forsythe Street in Beaumont in the late 1970s.
—Courtesy Chuck Little

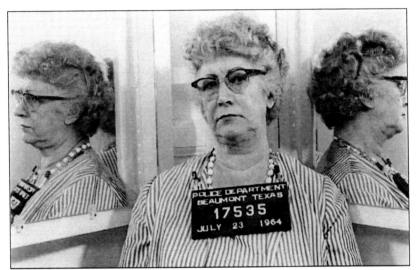

Mug shot of Rita Ainsworth at the Beaumont Police Department after her arrest at the Annex Apartments on July 23, 1964.

—Former Jefferson County Sheriff
R. E. "Dick" Culbertson papers, ms. 175,
Courtesy the Tyrrell Historical Library

Mug shot of an alleged prostitute at Rita Ainsworth's Lucas house on November 26, 1968.

—Former Jefferson County Sheriff
R. E. "Dick" Culbertson papers, ms. 175,
Courtesy the Tyrrell Historical Library

Rita Ainsworth pictured in 1964 at her home on Concord Road.
—The William H. McCain collection, file 1,
Courtesy the Tyrrell Historical Library

One of Rita Answorth's former "houses" in Vidor. Apparently Hurricane Rita, which hit the southeast Texas coast in the fall of 2005, decided this reminder of "days gone by" had been around long enough. She laid down her wrath in the form of trees smashing onto the roof. The owners later installed a generator that exploded and, as a result, the house burned to the ground.

—The Wanda A. Landrey collection,
Courtesy the Tyrrell Historical Library

PART VIII

Bringing Closure

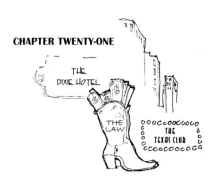

CHAPTER TWENTY-ONE

The Aftermath

In January 1971 Jefferson County District Attorney Tom Hanna filed a motion to dismiss 42 indictments returned in 1961, most of which arose from the vice cleanup. Criminal District Judge George Taylor signed the dismissals on January 22, which included five indictments against former Sheriff Charley Meyer, one against former Precinct 1 Constable Reagan Baker, 23 counts of gaming against Don Evans, Jr, and 12 counts of bribery involving N. H. Helms.

Hanna cited for his actions a 1969 U.S. Supreme Court ruling which held that efforts to pursue state charges over an eight-year period violated the Sixth Amendment of the U.S. Constitution. He also claimed "insufficiency of evidence" on which to base prosecutions.

"Let no person consider this action to be other than what it is," Hanna said in a prepared statement:

> It does not signal a return to the conditions that gave rise to these indictments, and this office will be just as vigorous in its attempts to suppress vice and official corruption as is necessary to see that [pre-1961] conditions do not return.
>
> This action merely recognizes the moral and professional duty of the district attorney's office to dismiss cases when the ends of

justice will best be served by such action and to go forward to matters which urgently need attention rather than looking backward to a period which we all sincerely hope we will never see again.[1]

Hanna's actions technically closed the doors on the pandemonium that reigned throughout the county after the Texas House Investigating Committee left the area ten years earlier. Despite the numerous indictments issued, and the overwhelming evidence that those involved in the scandal routinely accepted bribes to allow vice to exist, no officer or elected official implicated served any time in jail. The time had come, indeed, to move forward.

By 1971, Judge Owen Lord was deceased, and the remaining major participants in the vice campaign had gone and would continue to go in varied directions. After Sheriff Charley Meyer's defeat by R. E. "Dick" Culbertson in 1964, he retired to his childhood home in Ellinger, Texas. Bitter and professing that the vice cleanup "was one of the greatest setups of all times," he died in a nursing home in Bellville, Texas, in 1989 at the age of 76.[2]

District Attorney Ramie Griffin, who resigned from office in 1962, entered private practice in downtown Beaumont where he worked, still claiming to be the best gin rummy player in Jefferson County, until his death at 70 in 1983.[3]

Acting District Attorney W. G. "Gale" Walley ran unsuccessfully for the position of associate justice of the 9th District Court of Appeals in 1964, as well as for the 60th District Court bench in 1970. Tragically, he was found shot to death in his home on August 1, 1975, following a family quarrel with his wife.[4]

In 1977, Judge Harold Clayton stepped down from the 136th District Court, after accepting the appointment as an associate justice of the 9th District Court of Appeals by Governor Dolph Briscoe. He served in that capacity until September 30, 1983, retiring two years before his term expired.[5] In 1988 he and his wife moved to Wildwood, a community in Hardin County, where he lived until his death on October 1, 1991.[6]

Tom James, the young Texas legislator who came to Jefferson County in 1960 and upset the long-entrenched vice establishment, went on to lose the race for Texas attorney general in 1962.[7] He then practiced law in Dallas until his election in 1995 as an associate justice to the 5th District Court of Civil Appeals, a position he held until June 2004. After stepping down from the bench, Justice James moved to Celina, Texas, a small town 40 miles north of Dallas, where he continues to practice law.[8]

Now that more than forty years have passed since the vice cleanup, one of the most prophetic messages that appeared in the General Investigating Committee Report to the House of Representatives of the 57th Legislature of Texas still resounds clearly through the halls of justice. "Apathy, Bribery, Corruption. These are the ABC's of lawlessness. Decay is the next stage in the alphabetical progression."[9]

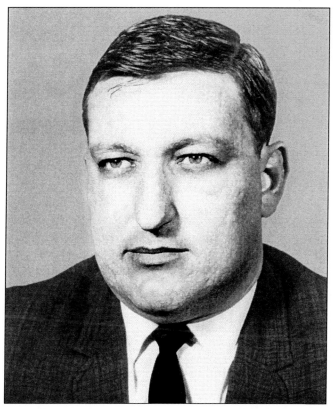

Former Jefferson County District Attorney Tom Hanna. In January 1971 Hanna filed a motion to dismiss 42 indictments returned in 1961. Criminal District Judge George Taylor signed the dismissals on January 22, 1971.

—Courtesy Tom Hanna

The new Crockett Street Entertainment District in Beaumont.

—The Wanda A. Landrey collection,
Courtesy the Tyrrell Historical Library

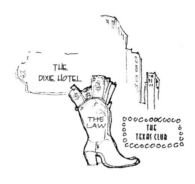

Afterword–
The Last Tour of the Dixie

On July 5, 2000, the day before the asbestos abatement project began on the Dixie Hotel, the owners of the Crockett Street Entertainment District granted me permission to walk through the building and take photographs. One of my guides was Mark Simmons, a project manager for Pneumatic Safety and Health Services. Jed Landrey, my son and owner of Inland Environments, the company hired to remove the asbestos, also escorted me through the Dixie. Although a grandmother and two young gentlemen were an unlikely threesome to be touring a brothel, I didn't care. This was historical research.

As we stood on the sidewalk before the tour began, we noticed that workers already had removed the brick wall that for years had covered the doors next to the entrance of the Dixie. We could see that the doors, now painted white, covered tinted glass underneath with white letters. At our request, a worker nearby scraped off enough paint for us to read the inscription: "Pipe Fitters Local 195." Very interesting!

We began our ascent up the stairway to the Dixie. Although I was hesitant to step on the fourth step in fear that I would set off the much-talked-about alarm buzzer, Mark assured me that the wiring had deteriorated long ago. After reaching the front entry-way, we turned to the left and saw the fire door that once separated the union hall from the brothel. Seeing the door only made me think: Did the wives of the union workers who lost their way into the Dixie ever wonder about the lengthy union meetings?

The hallway was dark and the air heavy as we retraced our steps back past the entryway. It soon became apparent that, except for the "Gone with the Wind" mural along the hallway and the dark-stained stairwell that led to the third floor, the long-ago grandeur had faded almost beyond recognition. As we continued our journey, my mind began to play tricks, and I started to experience visions from the past. . . .

"Here's Rita's apartment. Look! There's the air conditioning man holding a pillow case open, and Rita's filling it with five and ten dollar bills! I guess fives and tens are all she has in this place. But, what a way to pay for an expensive air-conditioning system.

"Let's go to the parlor. There's George Jones and some of the other guys flirting with the girls and playing the pinball machine! George better stop dallying with the girls and hurry on down to the street curb where he sings and plays his guitar. Who knows? Maybe he'll be famous one day. Now, who's that other guy trying to get a good feel?

"Oh, here's the buzzer control system that everyone's been talking about. I'll just push one of the buttons. My goodness, there's Mr. Smith! He's coming out of one of the rooms! Mr. Smith! Mr. Smith! I don't understand why he won't speak. He's always friendly when he sees me at church.

"OK, let's walk to the bar. I've heard that many of the young attorneys like to stop by for a drink after work. There they are, laughing and carrying on with the girls! But, they tell me they're really not interested in the girls. They just want a drink or two.

"Here's the back door with the peephole. Since this is the classiest brothel in town, Rita has to check everyone, because she allows only the blue bloods to come up. I'll just peep out to see if anyone's there on the stairway. Hi, come on in! You said you walked across the alley from the Beaumont Club and you only want to buy a drink? Perhaps I'm mistaken, but I thought surely they served plenty of drinks at the Beaumont Club. . . .

"OK, Mark and Jed, I've taken enough photos. Let's exit down the covered stairway leading to the back alley. You know there is a story that one rainy night before Rita built this canopy back in the 50s Mr. _____ slipped off the steps and broke his leg. He had a quick ride by ambulance to the hospital. Poor man, his wife never did feel sorry for him!"

As we walked along the dark and narrow alley behind the Dixie, I couldn't help but reminisce about the many colorful stories of hot times in early Jefferson County history. The gamblers, the madams, and the girls with hearts of gold left the red-light districts for greener pastures many years ago. The Dixie was about to become history, too.

The Jefferson County "District" Today

In 2003, with the completion of Rio Rita's Mexican Restaurant at 230 Crockett Street in Beaumont, the Crockett Street Development Corporation officially announced the completion of its Historic Crockett Street Entertainment District. As part of an urban renewal project, the corporation transformed the former businesses that once lined the 200 block of the street into entertainment venues. Now this area is one of the hottest nightspots in southeast Texas ... and everything is legal.

Should you ride in on a Harley, you may want to grab a snack and a "cool one" at Hog Wild; or, if you're hungry and not in the mood for tacos, try the Spindletop Restaurant. By then, you'll probably want to mosey on down the street to party the night away at some of the lively clubs and lounges. Just be sure to save some time for the Dixie Dance Hall. It's right where the Dixie Hotel and the Pipe Fitter's Local 195 union hall used to be. Once you arrive, you may walk around the hall and soak in a bit of nostalgia by viewing the infamous fire door that separated the two places, and Rita Ainsworth's outside peephole doors. Then, you may want to belly up to the bar where some of the original bedroom doors are set in panels. While there, be sure to cast your eyes to the northwest corner of the hall where you'll find a replica of one of the rooms. But, just remember, it's not for use. It's only a reminder of an era lost in time!

Many of the current establishments in the "district" are appointed in period decor, equally as fine as Rita's parlors of yesteryear. Some chronicle the history of Beaumont in sepia photos; others exhibit art as contemporary as music that drifts down the street on the wind. Bands play at street parties, while patrons sit under canopies enjoying the music and the pleasant atmosphere of downtown Beaumont. Whatever the occasion, Crockett Street now is a place to bring the family—yes, even the kids! The downtown renewal of the old district captures the spirit of days gone by and heralds the promise of better days yet to come in southeast Texas. But, as they say, old spirits never die. And lest we forget her name, was that Miss Rita blowing down Crockett Street on a hurricane?

Doors leading to the former Dixie Hotel and the former Pipe Fitters Local 195 union hall.

—The Wanda A. Landrey collection.
Courtesy the Tyrrell Historical Library

Jed Landrey, owner of Inland Environments, stands before steps leading to the front entrance of the Dixie Hotel.

—The Wanda A. Landrey collection,
Courtesy the Tyrrell Historical Library

The fire door between the former Pipe Fitters Local 195 union hall and the former Dixie Hotel.
—The Wanda A. Landrey collection.
Courtesy the Tyrrell Historical Library

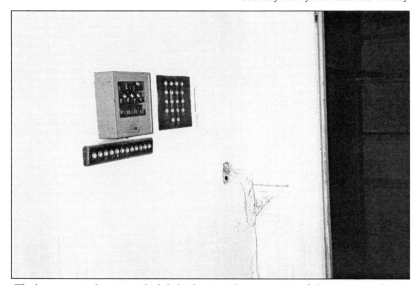

The buzzer control system, which helped protect the anonymity of the patrons at the Dixie.
—The Wanda A. Landrey collection,
Courtesy the Tyrrell Historical Library

The "Gone with the Wind" mural in the halls of the Dixie.
—The Wanda A. Landrey collection.
Courtesy the Tyrrell Historical Library

The stairwell leading to the upper floor of the Dixie.
—The Wanda A. Landrey collection,
Courtesy the Tyrrell Historical Library

The back door of the Dixie Hotel.
—The Wanda A. Landrey collection.
Courtesy theTyrrell Historical Library

During the 1950s, the Dixie Hotel was often referred to as the "Beaumont Club Annex" since some members of the club, which was located on the 6th floor of the Edson Hotel, would exit into the alleyway and use this covered stairwell to get to the back door of the Dixie.
—Courtesy *The Examiner*

Notes

Preface

1. Address by Attorney General Will Wilson to the United Citizens for Law Enforcement, Inc., Beaumont, Texas, August 22, 1961. Copy of address from the files of George Dishman, president of UCLE, 1961. Courtesy James Dishman, son of George Dishman; material in the possession of Wanda Landrey.

2. Ibid.

3. *Galveston: A History*, David McComb, University of Texas Press, 1986, p. 187.

4. Report of the General Legislative Investigating Committee of the House of Representatives on Law Enforcement in Jefferson County, April 7, 1961, 268-269, (hereafter cited as HGLIC Report).

5. HGLIC Report, 30-39.

6. Ibid., 250.

7. Walter Juncker, Beaumont CPA who served on the July 1960 term grand jury, telephone interview with Wanda Landrey, June 14, 2001.

Chapter One

1. David C. Humphrey, "Prostitution in Texas: From the 1830s to the 1960s," *East Texas Historical Journal*, Vol. XXXIII, p. 30.

2. Ibid., 31.

3. Ibid., 33-35.

4. Ibid., 36.

5. Robert F. Kennedy Memorial, 1367 Connecticut Avenue, N.W. Suite 200, Washington, D.C. 20036, www.RFKMemorial.org.

6. *Dallas News*, June 3, 1956.

7. *Galveston: A History*, David McComb, University of Texas Press, 1986, p. 186.

8. Ibid., 187.

9. Byron Fullerton, interoffice memo to Will Wilson, Attorney General's Office, January 27, 1958.

10. Tom James, former vice-chairman for the House General Investigating Committee, interview with Wanda Landrey, November 15, 1996, Dallas, Texas."

11. HGLIC, Report, 19.

Chapter Two

1. Jean and Gus McFaddin, owners of Plum Nearly Ranch, interview with Wanda Landrey, January 8, 2002, Beaumont, Texas.

2. HGLIC Report, 2-3.

3. Ibid., 1.

4. Attorney David Witts, former chief legal counsel for the House General Investigating Committee, interview with Wanda Landrey, May 1, 1997, Dallas, Texas.

5. HGLIC Report, 1.

6. Witts interview with Wanda Landrey, May 1, 1997. Dallas, Texas.

7. HGLIC Report, 3.

8. W. T. Wood, former assistant district attorney of Jefferson County, interview with Laura C. O'Toole, June 2, 1987, Beaumont, Texas.

9. HGLIC Report, 3.

10. Carrol Buttrill, former member of the United Citizens for Law Enforcement, interview with Wanda Landrey, February 1, 2002, Beaumont, Texas.

11. Raymond Lefkowitz, former freelance gambler and manager of the Balinese Club in Beaumont, interview with Wanda Landrey, August 30, 2001, Beaumont, Texas.

12. HGLIC Report, 2-3.

13. Charles Perricone, Beaumont police officer who served on the Special Services Vice Squad in the 1960s, interview with Wanda Landrey, March 10, 1997, Beaumont, Texas.

14. HGLIC Report, 3-5.

15. Joe Perl, Beaumont realtor and personal friend of Rita Ainsworth, interview with Wanda Landrey, June 29, 2001, Beaumont, Texas.

16. HGLIC Report, 3-4.

17. Ibid. 15.

Chapter Three

1. *Consumer Beacon*, February 1, 1978.

2. Wanda A. Landrey, *Outlaws in the Big Thicket*, (Austin: Eakin Press, 1976) p. 116.

3. *Consumer Beacon*, February 1, 1978.

4. *Beaumont Enterprise*, February 15, 1989.

5. Ibid., November 5, 2001.

6. R. E. "Dick" Culbertson, sheriff who succeeded Charley Meyer as sheriff of Jefferson County, interview with Wanda Landrey, July 11, 2000.

7. *Beaumont Enterprise*, October 1, 1961.

8. James interview with Wanda Landrey, November 15, 1996, Dallas, Texas.

9. Ramie Griffin, Jr., Beaumont attorney and son of Ramie Griffin, Sr., interview with Floyd Landrey, February 24, 2005, Beaumont, Texas.

10. Alfred S. Gerson, Judge of Jefferson County Court At Law No. 1, telephone interview with Wanda Landrey, January 18, 2005, Beaumont, Texas.

11. Ramie Griffin, Jr., interview with Floyd Landrey, February 24, 2005, Beaumont, Texas.

Chapter Four

1. *Beaumont Enterprise*, December 7, 1960.

2. Eugene Corder, Beaumont police officer who served on the Special Services Vice Squad in the early 1960s, interview with Wanda Landrey, May 22, 1997, Beaumont, Texas.

3. Ibid.

4. John Parsons, Beaumont police officer who served on the Special Services Vice Squad in the early 1960s, interview with Wanda Landrey, May 8, 1997, Lumberton, Texas.

5. HGLIC Report, 8-9.

6. Ibid., 10.

7. Ibid., 9.

8. Ibid.

9. Ibid.

10. Ibid., 9-10.

11. Ibid., 10.

12. Ibid., 11.

13. James interview with Wanda Landrey, November 15, 1996, Dallas, Texas.

14. HGLIC Report, 12-13.

15. Witts interview with Wanda Landrey, May 1, 1997, Dallas, Texas.

16. Lloyd G. Martin, former representative of the House General Investigating Committee, telephone interview with Wanda Landrey, November 14, 2001.

17. HGLIC Report, 10.

18. *Beaumont Enterprise*, December 21, 1960.

19. James interview with Wanda Landrey, November 15, 1996, Dallas, Texas.

20. HGLIC Report, 16-17.

21. Ibid., 17.

22. Martin telephone interview with Wanda Landrey, November 14, 2001.

Chapter Five

1. *Beaumont Daily Journal*, June 23, 1903.

2. Buster Turner, Beaumont police officer, interview with Wanda Landrey, June 27, 2001, Beaumont, Texas.

3. Buttrill interview with Wanda Landrey, February 1, 2002, Beaumont, Texas.

4. C. L. Pentecost, a Beaumont physician who treated Rita Ainsworth and some of her "girls," interview with Wanda Landrey, September 5, 2001, Beaumont, Texas.

5. Minni Palumbo Lindsey, Beaumont resident who lived at the edge of the early "red-light" district as a young girl, interview with Wanda Landrey, March 25, 2001, Beaumont, Texas.

6. Pentecost interview with Wanda Landrey, September 5, 2001, Beaumont, Texas.

7. Tanner Hunt, Beaumont attorney who represented Rita Ainsworth in the 1960s, interview with Wanda Landrey, June 21, 2001, Beaumont, Texas.

8. Ibid.

9. Turner interview with Wanda Landrey, June 27, 2001, Beaumont, Texas.

10. Smythe Sheperd, Beaumont businessman who lived near Charles Ainsworth's family as a boy, interview with Wanda Landrey, September 26, 2001, Beaumont, Texas.

11. Courtesy of Linda Hale, genealogist in Lumberton, Texas., record in the possession of Wanda Landrey.

12. Bruce Hamilton, former head of the Beaumont Historical Commission, interview with Wanda Landrey, January 24, 2002, Beaumont, Texas.

13. *The Examiner*, June 14-20, 2001.

14. Hamilton interview with Wanda Landrey, January 24, 2002, Beaumont, Texas.

15. Clyde Rush, former Beaumont assistant police chief, interview with Wanda Landrey, May 28, 1997, Beaumont, Texas.

16. Beaumont City Directory-1938. Nat A. Ainsworth listed as married to Claire with 2 children. (Claire was Rita Ainsworth's middle name). Jefferson County Divorce Records in the office of the District Clerk, Jefferson County, Texas., Cause No. 28755, styled Mary Ainsworth vs. Nat Ainsworth; Cause No. 47482, styled N. A. Ainsworth vs. Carrie Ainsworth; Cause No. 48641, styled Olive Knippel Ainsworth vs. N. A. Ainsworth.

17. Jefferson County Divorce Records in the office of the District Clerk, Jefferson County, Texas., Cause No. 48641, styled Olive Knippel Ainsworth vs. N. A. Ainsworth.

18. Beaumont City Directory-1943. Claire Ainsworth listed for the first time as Rita Ainsworth being in the soft drink business at 793 Bonham. Nat was listed as married to Claire.

19. Jefferson County Divorce Records in the office of the District Clerk, Jefferson County, Texas., Cause No. 8816-C, styled Rita Claire Ainsworth vs. Nat A. Ainsworth.

20. Ibid., Cause No. 8816-C, styled Rita Claire Ainsworth vs. Nat A. Ainsworth, Plaintiff's First Amended Petition, January 20, 1944; Plaintiff's

Second Amended Petition, May 10, 1944; Plaintiff's Third Amended Petition, October 25, 1944; Plaintiff's Fourth Amended Petition, November 20, 1944; Plaintiff's Fifth Amended Petition, January 16, 1945.

21. Probate Records in the office of the County Clerk, Jefferson County, Texas., Cause No. 10608, styled Estate of Nathaniel A. Ainsworth, Dec'd, filed May 20, 1947.

22. Bureau of Vital Statistics in the office of the County Clerk, Jefferson County, Texas., file No. 270, April 24, 1947.

23. Beaumont City Directory-1947. Rita Ainsworth was listed in a coin phonograph business at the New Blackstone Bar, 250½ Bowie.

24. Joe Dickerson, doctor who interned in Jasper, Texas, during the time that mock battles were taking place in Louisiana in preparation for the United States to enter WWII, interview with Wanda Landrey, January 27, 1996, Jasper, Texas.

25. David Sockler, Beaumont physician, interview with Wanda Landrey, March 19, 2002, Beaumont, Texas.

26. *Beaumont: A Chronicle of Promise*, Linsley, Judith Walker and Ellen Walker Rienstra, Woodland Hills: Windsor Publications, 1982, p. 114.

27. Report of the American Social Hygiene Assoc., New York, "Commercialized Prostitution Conditions in Beaumont, Texas.," December 1945 copy in the files of Wanda Landrey.

28. *Beaumont Enterprise*, October 4, 1987.

29. Mary Ellen Wisrodt, Beaumont resident, interview with Wanda Landrey, April 30, 2002, Beaumont, Texas.

30. Report of the American Social Hygiene Assoc., December 1945.

31. Ibid.

32. Ibid.

Chapter Six

1. Undated article, *Consumer Beacon*, in the files of Roy Dunn, Bridge City, Texas.

2. Hunt interview with Wanda Landrey, June 21, 2001, Beaumont, Texas.

3. Bobby Joe Henderson, former revenue officer for the IRS, interview with Wanda Landrey, November 5, 2001, Beaumont, Texas.

4. *Beaumont Sunday Enterprise-Journal*, November 9, 1980.

5. Hamilton interview with Wanda Landrey, January 24, 2002, Beaumont, Texas.

6. Perl interview with Wanda Landrey, June 29, 2001, Beaumont, Texas.

7. Hamilton interview with Wanda Landrey, January 24, 2002, Beaumont, Texas.

8. Deed Records in the office of the County Clerk, Jefferson County, Texas, Cause No. 189611, Vol. 639, pp. 571-572, filed October 8, 1946.

9. Perl interview with Wanda Landrey, June 29, 2001, Beaumont, Texas.

10. Ibid.

11. Hunt interview with Wanda Landrey, June 21, 2001, Beaumont, Texas.

12. R. T. Fertitta, Jr., former operator of the Elite Barber and Beauty Supply on Crockett Street in Beaumont, interview with Wanda Landrey, July 20, 2000, Beaumont, Texas.

13. Wisrodt interview with Wanda Landrey, April 30, 2002, Beaumont, Texas.

14. Mark Simmons, environmental consultant at the Crockett Street Entertainment District in Beaumont, interview with Wanda Landrey, July 5, 2000, Beaumont, Texas.

15. Fertitta interview with Wanda Landrey, July 20, 200, Beaumont, Texas.

16. Ibid.

17. Anonymous interview with Wanda Landrey, June 19, 2001, Beaumont, Texas.

18. Perl interview with Wanda Landrey, June 29, 2001, Beaumont, Texas.

19. Culbertson interview with Wanda Landrey, July 11, 2000.

20. Hunt interview with Wanda Landrey, June 21, 2001, Beaumont, Texas.

21. *The Examiner*, June 14-20, 2001.

22. *Cavalier*, "Through the Looking Glass with the Tall Americans," June 1962, p. 66.

23. Perl interview with Wanda Landrey, June 29, 2001, Beaumont, Texas.

24. Anonymous interview with Wanda Landrey, June 19, 2001, Beaumont, Texas.

25. Mary Lou Ainsworth, step-daughter of Rita Ainsworth, letter sent to Wanda Landrey, December 18, 2001.

26. Anonymous interview with Wanda Landrey, June 19, 2001, Beaumont, Texas.

27. Ibid.

28. Ibid.

29. Hunt interview with Wanda Landrey, June 21, 2001, Beaumont, Texas.

30. Ibid.

31. Dale Sheffield, former Beaumont resident who lived next to one of Rita Ainsworth's "girls" in the late 1940s, telephone interview with Wanda Landrey, June 14, 2001.

32. Anonymous interview with Wanda Landrey, June 19, 2001, Beaumont, Texas.

33. Ibid.

34. Parsons interview with Wanda Landrey, May 8, 1997, Lumberton, Texas.

35. Anonymous interview with Wanda Landrey, June 19, 2001, Beaumont, Texas.

36. Anonymous interview with Laura C. O'Toole, June 1987, Beaumont, Texas.

Chapter Seven

1. HGLIC Report, 68.
2. Hunt interview with Wanda Landrey, June 21, 2001, Beaumont, Texas.
3. Turner interview with Wanda Landrey, June 27, 2001, Beaumont, Texas.
4. HGLIC Report, 68.
5. Hunt interview with Wanda Landrey, June 21, 2001, Beaumont, Texas.
6. HGLIC Report, 68-69.
7. *Beaumont Enterprise*, July 4, 1958.
8. Jerry Conn interview with Laura C. O'Toole, March 5, 2003, Austin, Texas.
9. *Beaumont Enterprise*, October 11, 1964.
10. Jefferson County Trial Court Records of the Criminal District Court in the office of the District Clerk, Jefferson County, Texas, Trial Court No. 21841, styled State of Texas vs. Lee Wesley Marshall.
11. *Beaumont Enterprise*, October 11, 1964.
12. Ibid., April 22, 2002.
13. Ibid., July 26, 1942.
14. Jefferson County Trial Court Records of the Criminal District Court in the office of the District Clerk, Jefferson County, Texas, Trial Court No. 15, 383, styled State of Texas vs. Jerome A. Giles.
15. V. J. Barranco, owner of the Southwestern Printing Company in Beaumont, interview with Wanda Landrey, June 26, 2001, Beaumont, Texas.

Chapter Eight

1. Gilbert Alex, owner of Club Signature on Irving Street in Beaumont, interview with Wanda Landrey, August 28, 2001, Beaumont, Texas.
2. Ibid.
3. *Consumer Beacon*, "'Blue Buddy' Recalls Buddies & Blues,'" Vol. 1, No. 28, February 8, 1978.
4. Ibid.
5. Alex interview with Wanda Landrey, August 28, 2001, Beaumont, Texas.
6. Gabe Duriso, former waiter at Club Raven, interview with Wanda Landrey, August 28, 2001, Beaumont, Texas.
7. Corder interview with Wanda Landrey, May 22, 1997, Beaumont, Texas.
8. Reverend G. W. Daniels, pastor of the Sunlight Baptist Church in Beaumont, interview with Wanda Landrey, June 24, 1997, Beaumont, Texas.
9. Turner interview with Wanda Landrey, June 27, 2001, Beaumont, Texas.
10. HGLIC Report, p. 16.
11. Henderson interview with Wanda Landrey, November 5, 2001, Beaumont, Texas.
12. *Consumer Beacon*, February 8, 1978.
13. Daniels interview with Wanda Landrey, June 24, 1997, Beaumont, Texas.

Chapter Nine

1. Culbertson interview with Wanda Landrey, July 11, 2000, Beaumont, Texas.

2. Roy Dunn, owner of several area weekly newspapers, interview with Wanda Landrey, November 8, 2001, Bridge City, Texas.

3. Ibid.

4. D. P. Moore, former assistant chief of police in Port Arthur, interview with Wanda Landrey, May 6, 2001, Port Arthur, Texas.

5. Liz Hanna, resident of Port Arthur and area businesswoman, interview with Wanda Landrey, July 11, 2002, Beaumont, Texas.

6. Oliver "Sonny" Lawson, former resident and businessman of Port Arthur, interview with Wanda Landrey, October 1, 2000, Beaumont, Texas.

7. Terry Doyle, attorney in Port Arthur and former assistant district attorney, interview with Wanda Landrey, October 1, 2000, Beaumont, Texas.

8. Moore interview with Wanda Landrey, May 6, 2001, Port Arthur, Texas.

9. Lawson interview with Wanda Landrey, October 1, 2000, Beaumont, Texas.

10. Ibid.

11. Hilda Vickers, resident of Port Arthur, interview with Wanda Landrey, July 25, 2000, Port Arthur, Texas.

12. Ibid.

13. Hamilton interview with Wanda Landrey, January 24, 2002, Beaumont, Texas.

14. Anonymous interview with Wanda Landrey, June 19, 2001, Beaumont, Texas.

15. Sharon Woodyard Leamons, resident of Eugene, Oregon, and granddaughter of Grace Woodyard, telephone interview with Wanda Landrey, August 29, 2006; Pam Woodyard Escobedo, resident of San Diego, California, and relative of Grace Woodyard, e-mail correspondence with Wanda Landrey, August 29, 2006.

16. *Port Arthur Centennial History 1898-1998*, Looking Glass Media, in cooperation with Port Arthur Historical Society, 1997, pg. 428-29.

17. *Beaumont Enterprise*, February 19, 1989, Section C.

18. Joe Hughes, former school teacher and friend of Marcella Chadwell, interview with Wanda Landrey, January 9, 2003, Port Arthur, Texas.

19. Ibid.

20. *Steve McQueen, Portrait of an American Rebel,* Marshall Terrill, London: Plexus Publishing, 1993, p. 14.

21. Vickers interview with Wanda Landrey, July 25, 2000, Port Arthur, Texas.

22. Maudry DeWalt and Marie Price, daughters of Savannah Godeaux who owned a brothel in Port Arthur, interview with Wanda Landrey, October 11, 2001, Port Arthur, Texas.

23. Ibid., quotation by DeWalt.

24. Ibid., quotation by Price.

25. Ibid., quotation by DeWalt.

26. Ibid.

27. Ibid.

28. Ibid.

29. Ibid., quotation by Price.

30. Ibid.

31. Ibid.

Chapter Ten

1. Clyde Rush interview with Wanda Landrey, May 28, 1997, Beaumont, Texas.

2. Ibid.

3. HGLIC Report, 30.

4. Ibid., 30-39.

5. Ibid., 31.

6. George W. Parks, Jr., Beaumont businessman and member of the April 1955 term grand jury who helped found the Jefferson County Grand Jury Association, interview with Wanda Landrey, June 5, 1997, Beaumont, Texas.

7. Ibid.

8. Ibid.

9. Ibid.

10. Juncker telephone interview with Wanda Landrey, June 14, 2001.

11. Ibid.

12. HGLIC Report, 1.

13. James Barry, son of James C. "Huck" Barry who served on the July 1960 term grand jury, interview by Laura C. O'Toole, March 14, 1988, Lumberton, Texas.

14. *Beaumont Enterprise*, undated letter written by Evans Cappel, who served on the July 1960 term grand jury, to the editor of the newspaper; in the possession of Wanda Landrey.

Chapter Eleven

1. Erin Koenig, staff writer for the *Examiner*, interview with Wanda Landrey, June 2001, Beaumont, Texas.

2. HGLIC Report, 21.

3. Ibid., 22-29.

4. Ibid., 30-39.

5. Ibid., 47-51.

6. Ibid., 40.

7. Ibid., 40, Appendix C, six letters in a series of correspondence between Mrs. A.W. Lightfoot of Beaumont and the Office of The Attorney General in Austin. The letters cover the period from March 20, 1958, to January 19, 1959.

8. HGLIC Report, 52.

9. Ibid., 54.

10. James Vollers, former assistant district attorney, interview with Laura C. O'Toole, July 18, 1987, Austin, Texas.

11. HGLIC Report, 52.

12. Ibid., 67.

13. Ibid., 68-78.

14. Ibid., 80-83.

15. Ibid., 83-84.

16. Ibid., 85-95.

17. Ibid., 98-106.

18. Ibid., 98.

19. Ibid.

20. Ibid., 96-98.

21. Ibid., 116.

22. Ibid., 138.

23. Ibid., 120-124.

24. Ibid., 124-131.

25. Ibid., 132-137.

26. Ibid., 148.

27. Ibid., 149.

28. Ibid., 149-151.

29. Ibid., 151-173.

30. Ibid., 173-179, 179-181.

31. Ibid., 202-226.

32. Ibid., 226-233.

33. Ibid., 233-248.

34. Ibid., 181-197.

35. Ibid., 197.

36. Carl Kohler, interview with Laura C. O'Toole, June 1, 1987, Beaumont, Texas.

37. HGLIC Report, 197-201.

38. Ibid., 251-252.

39. Ibid., 252-255.

40. Ibid., 255-256.

41. Ibid., 256-257.

Chapter Twelve

1. *Beaumont Journal*, January 7, 1961.

2. *Beaumont Enterprise*, January 7, 1961.

3. Ibid.

4. Ibid.

5. Ibid., January 11, 1961.

6. Hamilton interview with Wanda Landrey, January 24, 2002.

7. *Beaumont Enterprise*, January 11, 1961.

8. Ibid., January 14, 1961.

9. Ibid., January 11, 1961.

10. *Beaumont Journal*, February 10, 1961.

11. *Stafford v. Firemen's and Policemen's Civil Service Commission of the City of Beaumont*, 355 S.W.2d 555 (Tex. Civ. App.- Beaumont 1962, writ affirmed).

12. *Beaumont Enterprise*, January 12, 1961.

13. Ibid., January 16, 1961.

14. *Beaumont Journal*, January 16, 1961.

15. Ibid., January 16, 1961.

16. *Beaumont Enterprise*, January 18, 1961.

17. Ibid., February 3, 1961.

18. Bishop John Wesley Hardt, former pastor of the First United Methodist Church in Beaumont, interview with Wanda Landrey, May 21, 1997, Dallas, Texas.

19. *Beaumont Enterprise*, January 18, 1961.

20. Hardt interview with Wanda Landrey, May 21, 1997, Dallas, Texas.

Chapter Thirteen

1. United Citizens for Law Enforcement (hereafter cited as UCLE), First Annual Report, 1961.

2. *Beaumont Journal*, January 20, 1961.

3. UCLE, First Annual Report, 1961.

4. *Beaumont Journal*, January 20, 1961.

5. UCLE, First Annual Report, 1961.

6. *Beaumont Enterprise*, March 10, 1961.

7. Ibid., February 11, 1961.

8. *Beaumont Journal*, March 9, 1961.

9. Ibid., March 15, 1961.

10. Robert Q. Keith, former Beaumont attorney who assisted his father Quentin Keith in the representation of Ramie Griffin in the early 1960s, telephone interview with Wanda Landrey, December 18, 2003.

11. *Beaumont Enterprise*, March 14, 1961.

12. *Beaumont Journal*, March 15, 1961.

Chapter Fourteen

1. *Beaumont Enterprise*, January 13, 1961.

2. Perricone interview with Wanda Landrey, March 10, 1997, Beaumont, Texas.

3. Parsons interview with Wanda Landrey, May 8, 1997, Lumberton, Texas.

4. Ibid.

5. Perricone interview with Wanda Landrey, March 10, 1997, Beaumont, Texas.

6. Parsons interview with Wanda Landrey, May 8, 1997, Lumberton, Texas.

Chapter Fifteen

1. *Beaumont Enterprise*, January 19, 1961.

2. Ibid. January 13, 1961.

3. Ibid., January 28, 1961; Judge James Farris, former assistant district attorney of Jefferson County, interview with Wanda Landrey, February 13, 2002, Beaumont, Texas.

4. Parsons interview with Wanda Landrey, May 8, 1997, Lumberton, Texas.

5. *Beaumont Journal*, February 2, 1961.

6. *Beaumont Enterprise*, March 16, 1961.

7. Ibid.

8. Ibid., March 17, 1961.

9. UCLE, First Annual Report, 1961.

10. *Beaumont Enterprise*, March 16, 1961.

11. *Beaumont Journal*, March 27, 1961.

12. *Beaumont Enterprise*, March 29, 1961.

13. Final Report of the Jefferson County Criminal Court Grand Jury for the January term, 1961, in the office of the District Clerk, Jefferson County, Texas.

14. Final Report of the Jefferson County Criminal Court Grand Jury for the April term, 1961, in the office of the District Clerk, Jefferson County, Texas.

15. UCLE, First Annual Report, 1961.

16. Final Report of the Jefferson County Criminal Court Grand Jury for the April term, 1961, in the office of the District Clerk, Jefferson County, Texas.

17. The *Houston Post*, "Beaumont Used To Push Kennedy Anti-Crime Bill, May 18, 1961; UCLE, First Annual Report, 1961.

18. UCLE, First Annual Report, 1961.

19. *The American Weekly*, a supplement to the *Houston Chronicle*, October 8, 1961.

20. *Time*, January 12, 1962.

21. *Cavalier*, "Through the Looking Glass with the TALL Americans," June, 1962.

Chapter Sixteen

1. *Beaumont Journal*, July 3, 1961.

2. *Beaumont Enterprise*, July 9, 1961.

3. Ibid., July 11, 1961.

4. Parsons interview with Wanda Landrey, May 8, 1997, Lumberton, Texas.

5. UCLE, Second Annual Report, 1962. Copy from the files of George

Dishman, president of UCLE, 1961; material in the possession of Wanda Landrey.

6. Parsons interview with Wanda Landrey, May 8, 1997, Lumberton, Texas.

7. UCLE, Second Annual Report, 1962.

8. UCLE, Second Annual Report, 1962; UCLE, Third Annual Report, 1963; material in the possession of Wanda Landrey.

9. Lefkowitz interview with Wanda Landrey, August 30, 2001, Beaumont, Texas.

10. Ibid.

11. Parsons interview with Wanda Landrey, May 8, 1997, Lumberton, Texas.

Chapter Seventeen

1. *Beaumont Enterprise*, July 23, 1961.

2. *Port Arthur News*, July 12, 1961.

3. *Beaumont Enterprise*, July 20, 1961.

4. Ibid., July 23, 1961.

5. Ibid.

6. Ibid., August 1, 1961.

7. *Houston Chronicle*, article written by Sara Marsteller, *Chronicle* Correspondent, August 2, 1961.

8. *Beaumont Enterprise*, August 2, 1961.

9. *Houston Chronicle*, August 2, 1961.

10. *The Verdict*, newsletter published by the Citizens for Democratic Law and Order, August 1961. Copy from the files of George Dishman; material in the possession of Wanda Landrey.

Chapter Eighteen

1. *Beaumont Enterprise*, September 19, 1961.

2. Special Report of the Jefferson County Criminal Court Grand Jury for the July term, 1961, in the office of the District Clerk, Jefferson County, Texas.

3. *Beaumont Enterprise*, September 27, 1961.

4. Ibid.

5. Undated letter addressed to the Office of the Criminal District Attorney of Jefferson County, Texas., from H. M. Nix, Jr., foreman of the July term, 1961, Criminal Court Grand Jury; letter in the possession of Wanda Landrey.

6. *Beaumont Enterprise*, September 29, 1961.

7. Ibid., September 30, 1961.

8. Ibid., October 1, 1961.

9. Ibid., November 2, 1961.

10. Ibid.

11. Ibid., November 4, 1961.

12. UCLE, First Annual Report, 1961.

13. *Beaumont Enterprise*, December 1, 1961.

14. Ibid., December 2, 1961; copy of Clayton's statement from the files of George Dishman; material in the possession of Wanda Landrey.

15. *Beaumont Enterprise*, December 6, 1961.

16. Ibid., December 12, 1961.

17. Ibid., December 14, 1961.

18. Ibid., December 15, 1961.

19. Ibid., December 16, 1961.

20. Ibid., December 20, 1961.

21. Ibid., December 21, 1961.

22. Ibid., December 29, 1961.

23. Ibid., December 30, 1961.

24. Final Report of the Jefferson County 136th District Court Grand Jury for the July term, 1961, in the office of the District Clerk, Jefferson County, Texas.

25. *Beaumont Enterprise*, December 30, 1961; *Houston Chronicle*, article written by Sara Marsteller, *Chronicle* correspondent, December 31, 1961.

26. *Beaumont Enterprise*, December 31, 1961.

27. Ibid., January 11, 1962.

28. *Beaumont Enterprise*, December 22, 1961.

29. Ibid.

30. Ibid., December 31, 1961.

31. Ibid.

Chapter Nineteen

1. William B. Hataway, member of the January term, 1962, 136th District Court Grand Jury, interview with Wanda Landrey, July 31, 2000, Beaumont, Texas.

2. Final reports of the Jefferson County Criminal District Court Grand Jury and the 136th District Court Grand Jury for the January term, 1962, in the office of the District Clerk, Jefferson County, Texas.; *Beaumont Enterprise*, January 17, 1962.

3. *Beaumont Enterprise*, March 20, 1962.

4. Ibid., March 3, 1962.

5. Ibid., May 6, 1962.

6. UCLE, Second Annual Report, 1962.

7. Ibid.

8. UCLE, Third Annual Report, 1963.

9. *Beaumont Enterprise*, April 6, 1963.

10. UCLE, Third Annual Report, 1963.

11. *Beaumont Enterprise*, October 4, 1963.

12. Jo Culbertson, wife of former Jefferson County Sheriff R. E. "Dick" Culbertson, interview with Wanda Landrey, July 11, 2000, Beaumont, Texas.

13. R. E. "Dick" Culbertson interview with Wanda Landrey, July 11, 2000.

14. *Beaumont Enterprise*, May 3, 1964.

Chapter Twenty

1. Pentecost interview with Wanda Landrey, February 1, 2002, Beaumont, Texas.

2. Undated article, "Stay Out of Orange, Vice Characters Told," *Houston Chronicle*, in the possession of former representative Lloyd G. Martin, and in the files of Wanda Landrey.

3. C. E. "Pete" Landolt, former city councilman of Silsbee, Texas, interview with Wanda Landrey, January 7, 2003, Kountze, Texas.

4. Henderson interview with Wanda Landrey, November 5, 2001.

5. Cecil Rush, Beaumont police officer who served on the Special Services Vice Squad in the 1960s, interview with Wanda Landrey, September 11, 2001, Beaumont, Texas.

6. Corder interview with Wanda Landrey, May 22, 1997, Beaumont, Texas.

7. Parsons interview with Wanda Landrey, May 8, 1997, Lumberton, Texas.

8. Perricone interview with Wanda Landrey, March 10, 1997, Beaumont, Texas.

9. Doyle interview with Wanda Landrey, October 1, 2000, Beaumont, Texas.

10. Parsons interview with Wanda Landrey, May 8, 1997, Lumberton, Texas.

11. Corder interview with Wanda Landrey, May 22, 1997, Beaumont, Texas.

12. Perricone interview with Wanda Landrey, March 10, 1997, Beaumont, Texas.

13. *Savor*, supplement to the *Beaumont Enterprise*, November 2001.

14. *Beaumont Journal*, August 25, 1980.

15. *Savor*, November 2001.

16. Charles W. "Chuck" Little, Beaumont Police officer who led in the arrests of a prostitution and drug operation on Forsythe Street in Beaumont in the late 1970s, interview with Wanda Landrey, April 7, 2002, Lumberton, Texas.

17. Doyle interview with Wanda Landrey, October 1, 2000, Beaumont, Texas.

Chapter Twenty-one

1. Tom Hanna, former district attorney of Jefferson County, interview with Wanda Landrey, July 11, 2002, Beaumont Texas; *Beaumont Journal*, January 23, 1971.

2. *Beaumont Enterprise*, January 7, 1996.

3. Ramie Griffin, Jr., Beaumont attorney, interview with Floyd Landrey, February 3, 2005.

4. *Beaumont Enterprise*, August 2, 1975.

5. *Beaumont Enterprise*, August 24, 1983.

6. Robbie Graham, resident of Wildwood addition in Hardin County, telephone interview with Wanda Landrey, March 1, 2005.

7. *Beaumont Enterprise*, January 7, 1996.

8. James telephone interview with Wanda Landrey, April 11, 2005.

9. HGLIC Report, 268.

Bibliography

Books

Beaumont City Directory. Houston: Morrison & Fourmy Directory Co., 1938-1947.

Landrey, Wanda A. *Outlaws in the Big Thicket*. Austin: Eakin Press, 1976.

Linsley, Judith Walker, and Rienstra, Ellen Walker. *Beaumont: A Chronicle of Promise*. Woodland Hills, California: Windsor Publications, 1982.

McComb, David. *Galveston: A History*. Austin: University of Texas Press, 1984.

Port Arthur Centennial History 1898-1998. Looking Glass Media, in cooperation with Port Arthur Historical Society, 1997.

South Western Reporter, Second Series. St. Paul: West Publishing Company, 1962.

Terrill, Marshall. *Steve McQueen, Portrait of an American Rebel*. London: Plexus Publishing, 1993.

Newspapers and Magazines

American Weekly, supplement to the *Houston Chronicle*, October 8, 1961.

Beaumont Daily Journal, June 23, 1903.

Beaumont Enterprise, July 26, 1942–February 19, 1989.

Beaumont Journal, January 7, 1961–August 25, 1980.

Cavalier Magazine, June 1962.

Consumer Beacon, February 1, 1978; February 8, 1978.

Examiner, June 14-20, 2001.

Houston Chronicle, August 2, 1961–December 31, 1961.

Houston Post, January 14, 1961–May 18, 1961.

Port Arthur News, July 12, 1961.

Savor, supplement to the *Beaumont Enterprise*, November 2001.

Time Magazine, January 12, 1962.

Verdict, August 1961.

Records

County Court Records, Office of the County Clerk, Jefferson County Courthouse, Beaumont, Texas.

District Court Records, Office of the District Clerk, Jefferson County Courthouse, Beaumont, Texas.

Theses

Cerniglia, Laura Kathleen (O'Toole). "Purging a Corrupt Government: The Clean-up of Jefferson County." Bachelor's honors thesis. University of Texas, Austin, Texas, 1988.

Reports

American Social Hygiene Association, Incorporated, New York, report on "Commercialized Prostitution Conditions in Beaumont, Texas, 1945. Copy in possession of Wanda Landrey.

General Investigating Committee Report to the House of Representatives of the 57th Legislature of Texas, Jefferson County Investigation, Austin, Texas.

United Citizens For Law Enforcement, Inc. Annual Reports, 1961-1963. Copies in possession of Wanda Landrey.

Letters

Mary Lou Ainsworth, step-daughter of Rita Ainsworth, to Wanda Landrey, December 18, 2001. In possession of Wanda Landrey.

H. M. Nix, Jr., foreman of the July term, 1961, Criminal Court Grand Jury, to the Office of the Criminal District Attorney of Jefferson County, Texas. Copy in possession of Wanda Landrey.

Interviews

Alex, Gilbert. Interview with Wanda Landrey, Beaumont, Texas, August 28, 2001.

Anonymous. Interview with Wanda Landrey, Beaumont, Texas, June 19, 2001.

Anonymous. Interview with Laura C. O'Toole, Beaumont, Texas, June 12, 1987.

Asta, Anthony. Telephone interview with Wanda Landrey, May 3, 2005.

Barranco, V. J. Interview with Wanda Landrey, Beaumont, Texas, June 26, 2001.

Barry, James. Interview with Laura C. O'Toole, Lumberton, Texas, March 14, 1988.

Baxter, Gordon. Interview with Laura C. O'Toole, Beaumont, Texas, June 6, 1987.

Buser, Steve. Interview with Wanda Landrey, Beaumont, Texas, February 22, 2005.

Buttril, Carrol. Interview with Wanda Landrey, Beaumont, Texas, February 1, 2001.

Campbell, William R. "Rusty." Interview with Wanda Landrey, Beaumont, Texas, June 19, 2001.

Conn, Jerry. Interview with Laura C. O'Toole, Austin, Texas, March 5, 2003.

Corder, Eugene. Interview with Wanda Landrey, Beaumont, Texas, May 22, 1997.

Culbertson, R. E. "Dick." Interview with Wanda Landrey, Beaumont, Texas, July 11, 2000.

Interview with Laura C. O'Toole, Beaumont, Texas, November 6, 1987.

Culbertson, Jo. Interview with Wanda Landrey, Beaumont, Texas, July 11, 2000.

Daniels, Reverend G. W. Interview with Wanda Landrey, Beaumont, Texas, June 24, 1997.

DeWalt, Maudry. Interview with Wanda Landrey, Port Arthur, Texas, October 11, 2001.

Doyle, Terry. Interview with Wanda Landrey, Beaumont, Texas, October 1, 2000.

Dunn, Roy. Interview with Wanda Landrey, Bridge City, Texas, November 8, 2001.

Duriso, Gabe. Interview with Wanda Landrey, Beaumont, Texas, August 28, 2001.

Escobedo, Pam Woodyard. E-mail interview with Wanda Landrey, August 29, 2006.

Farris, James. Interview with Wanda Landrey, Beaumont, Texas, February 13, 2002.

Farrow, L. D. Interview with Wanda Landrey, Nederland, Texas, May 22, 2001.

Fertitta, R. T., Jr. Interview with Wanda Landrey, Beaumont, Texas, July 20, 2000.

Frank, Mike. Interview with Laura C. O'Toole, May 12, 2003.

Gerson, Al. Telephone interview with Wanda Landrey, January 18, 2005.

Graham, Robbie. Telephone interview with Wanda Landrey, March 14, 2005.

Greer, Jeanette. Interview with Wanda Landrey, Beaumont, Texas, April 17, 2003.

Griffin Jr., Ramie. Interview with Floyd Landrey, Beaumont, Texas, February 24, 2005.

Hale, Linda. Telephone interview with Wanda Landrey, January 18, 2005.

Hamilton, Bruce. Interview with Wanda Landrey, Beaumont, Texas, January 24, 2002.

Hanna, Liz. Interview with Wanda Landrey, Beaumont, Texas, July 11, 2002.

Hanna, Tom. Interview with Wanda Landrey, Beaumont, Texas, July 11, 2002.

Hardt, Bishop John Wesley. Interview with Wanda Landrey, Dallas, Texas, May 21, 1997.

Hataway, William B. Interview with Wanda Landrey, Beaumont, Texas, July 31, 2000.

Hawkes, C. Keith. Interview with Wanda Landrey, Beaumont, Texas, March 8, 2005.

Henderson, Bobby Joe. Interview with Wanda Landrey, Beaumont, Texas, November 5, 2001.

Holstead, Cecil. Interview with Wanda Landrey, Port Neches, Texas, June 29, 2000.

Hughes, Joe. Interview with Wanda Landrey, Port Arthur, Texas, January 9, 2003.

Hunt, Tanner. Interview with Wanda Landrey, Beaumont, Texas, June 29, 2001.

James, Tom. Interview with Wanda Landrey, Dallas, Texas, November 15, 1996. Telephone interview, April 11, 2005. Interview with Laura C. O'Toole, Dallas, Texas, February 19, 1988.

Juncker, Walter. Telephone interview with Wanda Landrey, June 14, 2001.

Keith, Robert Q. Telephone interview with Wanda Landrey, December 18, 2003.

King, Jack. Interview with Wanda Landrey, Beaumont, Texas, May 7, 2002.

King, Melissa Ann. Interview with Wanda Landrey, Beaumont, Texas, July 2, 2001.

Koenig, Erin. Interview with Wanda Landrey, Beaumont, Texas, June, 2001.

Kohler, Carl. Interview with Laura C. O'Toole, Beaumont, Texas, June 1, 1987.

Landolt, C. E. "Pete." Interview with Wanda Landrey, Kountze, Texas, January 7, 2003.

Lawson, Oliver "Sonny." Interview with Wanda Landrey, Beaumont, Texas, October 1, 2000.

Leamons, Sharon Woodyard. Telephone interview with Wanda Landrey, August 29, 2006.

Lefkowitz, Raymond. Interview with Wanda Landrey, Beaumont, Texas, August 30, 2001.

Lester, Julia. Interview with Wanda Landrey, Lumberton, Texas, January 3, 2003.

Lindsey, Minnie Palumbo. Interview with Wanda Landrey, Beaumont, Texas, March 25, 2001.

Little, Charles W. "Chuck." Interview with Wanda Landrey, Lumberton, Texas, April 7, 2002.

Locke, Helen. Interview with Wanda Landrey, Beaumont, Texas, April 17, 2003.

Lord, Evelyn. Interview with Wanda Landrey, Beaumont, Texas, February 23, 2005.

McFaddin, Jean and Gus. Interview with Wanda Landrey, Beaumont, Texas, January 8, 2002.

McGrath, James. Interview with Wanda Landrey, Beaumont, Texas, February 24, 1997.

Martin, Lloyd G. Telephone interview with Wanda Landrey, November 14, 2001.

Moore, D. P. Interview with Wanda Landrey, Port Arthur, Texas, May 6, 2001.

Moore, Ray. Interview with Wanda Landrey, Crested Butte, Colorado, August 6, 2001.

Nix, H. M., Jr. Interview with Wanda Landrey, Beaumont, Texas, July 15, 2002.

Parks, George W. Interview with Wanda Landrey, Beaumont, Texas, June 5, 1997.

Parsons, John. Interviews with Wanda Landrey, Lumberton, Texas, May 8 and July 11, 1997.

Pentecost, C. L. Interview with Wanda Landrey, Beaumont, Texas, September 5, 2001.

Perl, Joe. Interview with Wanda Landrey, Beaumont, Texas, June 29, 2001.

Perricone, Charles. Interview with Wanda Landrey, Beaumont, Texas, March 10, 1997.

Price, Marie. Interview with Wanda Landrey, Port Arthur, Texas, October 11, 2001.

Reid, Bill. Interview with Wanda Landrey, Beaumont, Texas, December 13, 2001.

Rush, Cecil. Interview with Wanda Landrey, Beaumont, Texas, September 11, 2001.

Rush, Clyde. Interview with Wanda Landrey, Beaumont, Texas, May 28, 1997.

Sheffied, Dale. Telephone interview with Wanda Landrey, June 14, 2001.

Sheperd, Smythe. Interview with Wanda Landrey, Beaumont, Texas, September 26, 2001.

Simmons, Mark. Interview with Wanda Landrey, Beaumont, Texas, July 5, 2000.

Sockler, David. Interview with Wanda Landrey, Beaumont, Texas, March 19, 2002.

Turner, Buster. Interview with Wanda Landrey, Beaumont, Texas, June 27, 2001.

VanZandt, Ed. Interview with Wanda Landrey, Beaumont, Texas, July 7, 2001.

Vickers, Hilda. Interview with Wanda Landrey, Port Arthur, Texas, July 25, 2000.

Vollers, James. Interview with Laura C. O'Toole, Austin, Texas, July 18, 1987.

Walker, Charles. Interview with Wanda Landrey, Beaumont, Texas, May 7, 1998.

Wilson, Will. Interview with Laura C. O'Toole, Austin, Texas, April 4, 1987.

Wisrodt, Mary Ellen. Interview with Wanda Landrey, Beaumont, Texas, April 30, 2002.

Witts, David. Interview with Wanda Landrey, Dallas, Texas, May 1, 1997.

Interview with Laura C. O'Toole, Dallas, Texas, February 18, 1988.

Index

About the Authors

WANDA CRUSE LANDREY, a native of Beaumont and a descendant of early East Texas pioneers, is a historian, writer, and researcher with experience in on-site documentation of regional history. She has traveled extensively in her pursuit of stories of the people of southeast Texas. In addition to *Betting, Booze, and Brothels: Vice, Corruption, and Justice in Jefferson County, Texas, from Spindletop to the 1960s,* Ms. Landrey is the author of five other books: *Outlaws in the Big Thicket, Boardin' in the Thicket: Reminiscences and Recipes of Early Big Thicket Boarding Houses, The Historic Belle-Jim Hotel,* and two children's novels, *Lost in the Big Thicket* and *The Ghosts of Spindletop Hill.* She was recognized in 2002 by the Hardin County Historical Commission for her service in the preservation of Big Thicket folklore, and in 1990 received a citation award from the San Antonio Conservation Society for *Boardin' in the Thicket.* The book later was selected to be among those featured in the cookbook *Best of the Best from Texas II.* She holds B.A. and M.A. degrees from Lamar University in Beaumont.

The 1997 Beaumont Independent School District's featured author during National Childrens Book Week, Ms. Landrey is presently conducting interviews with Texas lawyers across the state and donating copies to the archives of the State Board of Texas.

Ms. Landrey is a mother and grandmother and resides in Beaumont with her husband, Floyd A. Landrey, of the Moore, Landrey law firm.

LAURA CERNIGLIA O'TOOLE was born and raised in Beaumont. Her family roots extend far into East Texas as well. She fondly remembers sitting in the kitchen of her grandmother, Earlene Dehart Rosser, listening to tales about life in the Big Thicket. She was especially inspired by stories about her great uncle, Whit Whitaker, who was the sheriff of Hardin County during the fifties and sixties.

Ms. O'Toole attended the University of Texas and graduated with a B.A. from the Plan II Honors Program in 1988. Ms. O'Toole first wrote about the James Commission investigation in her thesis entitled "Purging a Corrupt Government: The Clean-up of Jefferson County," for which she received Special Honors.

Ms. O'Toole graduated from the University of Texas School of Law in 1991. She practices law in Austin where she lives with her husband, Brian, and their two daughters. This is her first book.